This book
purchased
with donations
made to the
GiveBIG
for Books
Campaign.

W•CLARK
PUBLISHING

Mama
Jones

MY GUIDE TO LOVE &
Romance

Mama Jones
Guide to Love & Romance!

Wahida Clark Presents Publishing
60 Evergreen Place
Suite 904
East Orange, New Jersey 07018
973-678-9982
www.wclarkpublishing.com

Mama Jones: My Guide to Love and Romance **by** Nancy 'Mama' Jones
ISBN 13-digit 978-1936649655
ISBN 10-digit 1936649659

Library of Congress Cataloging-In-Publication Data:
LCCN 2013914912
1. Relationships 2. African American   3. Relationship Advice
4. Love and Romance 5. Reality Television   6. Motivational
7. Love and Hip Hop   8. Marriage   9. Spiritual

Cover design and layout by Nuance Art, LLC
Book design by NuanceArt@gmail.com
Proofreader Rosalind Hamilton
Sr. Editor Alah Adams
Sr. Editor Linda Wilson

Mama Jones
My Guide to Love & Romance

Mama Jones
My Guide to Love & Romance

Mama's Dedication Page

Dedicated to my Son Jim, My Grandsons, Vaun and the rest of the men in my life.

Mama Jones
My Guide to Love & Romance

Mama Jones
My Guide to Love & Romance

Acknowledgements From Mama

You know I have to thank God first because all things are possible with him! To my mother Sally Jones (The Pum'Kásh) and Father Nelson Jones (The Peré deux ché), without you both I wouldn't have been able to even be here. My son Jelmoe has always been my biggest supporter, and still is! Check me out now I have a book; you're next.

To my daughters; Alcua, Jamila, Precious, Khadija & Alexis, I want to thank you for being one of the inspirations for writing this book. The teachings in this book should not come to you as a surprise because I have guided you all on 'Love & Romance'. My nephew Shawn and my brother Ricky the two other men in my life thank you for grinding it out with me always.

Special thanks to Collette Bonaparte for this glamorous cover photo of myself! I look like a million bucks girl! To my devoted impeccable got damn team that have been holding me down; KC Rosa, Donna Scott, Karif Knox, Latoya 'Sassy' E.,

Mama Jones
My Guide to Love & Romance

Terrell S. Everett, and Alexis again, I thank ya . . . they said scared money don't make money, now let's make some more! Also, I would like to thank the editor's Alah Adams and Linda Wilson of this project who did a phenomenal job and put in lots of hard work.

And finally, the publisher Ms. Wahida Clark and your team at Wahida Clark Presents Publishing, you and your staff helped bring *My Guide to Love and Romance* to life and I will always love and thank you for that.

Ciao!

WAHIDA CLARK PRESENTS

Mama Jones

MY GUIDE TO LOVE &

Romance

My Guide to Love & Romance

Introduction

Hey, it's me Nancy Jones, better known to the world as Mama Jones of *Love & Hip Hop* and *Chrissy & Mr. Jones* reality TV shows. I'm also Hip Hop's favorite mother. If you don't know, you better ask somebody! I've done two seasons of *Love & Hip Hop*, two seasons of *Chrissy & Mr. Jones*, and I am also working on my own show *Mama Jones's World* , make sure you stay tuned. I'm very excited, as you should be, because let me tell you something. You haven't been entertained like this, EVER!

I've been on this earth fifty-four years to the date (yeah, yeah, I know I look good for my age), so that qualifies me as a veteran of life. Once you pass fifty, you're somewhat of an expert at just simply living. I'm the mother of five children, and I've been married three times. I've also had countless men trying to get with me. You want to know why? Because I know a few things about Love & Romance, things that most of you young whipper-snappers wish you knew. There are some things I'm going to teach that I wish I knew when I was young. Then I wouldn't have made so many mistakes in the relationship department before I finally got it right. But I have been blessed, and it's my sincere and humble intention to pass on those blessings to you through this book. There is a little something in this guide for both genders. My purpose for writing this book is to bless the youth with some good wisdom that will enhance their existence, but I'm also writing *Mama Jones' Guide to Love & Romance* for all humanity.

You see, most of you know me from reality TV, and as mother to rap star, Jim Jones. You want to know something? I didn't choose reality TV. Reality TV chose me! I was minding my business when my son recommended me. The producers wanted someone on the show that was off the chain, so my son said, "My mother is who you need to get on the show." They interviewed me and the rest is history.

Yeah, I'm as real as they come, but everything on that show doesn't represent the real me all the time. That would be impossible! I can say a whole paragraph, and after they finish editing it, all you get is one sentence. If you want to know the real me, reading this book is about as close as you're going to

My Guide to Love & Romance

get without being all up in my damn face. What most of you don't know about me is that I am what they call a *Hopeless Romantic*. Yes, Mama Jones loves her some Romance, but first and foremost I believe in God. Second, I believe in the power of LOVE. I'm going to tell you something my dear grandmother (God rest her soul) told me when I was a young woman. "Love is not supposed to hurt." She said, "When you Love yourself, then a man will Love you." Those wise words stuck with me throughout my life. When I finally got it right is when I finally got me right. Now it's time to get you right.

Although this guide is written for every adult, young and old. I have to begin with the most dire circumstances. Today I truly believe the future of Black relationships is at stake. This is a serious issue that requires careful introspection. When there is more Black on Black crime than there is Black on Black Love, not only is our future at risk, but our present looks devastatingly bleak.

According to a National Health Statistics report titled *First Marriages in the United States: Data from 2006 through 2010 National Survey of Family Growth,* Black women 18 to 44 have the lowest percentage of first marriages at only 26%, which is 6% lower than Black men who are currently married. First marriages for White women in that same age group is at

My Guide to Love & Romance

51%, almost double that of the Black woman! I'm not hating on my White sisters, but I know about half of those marriages are probably to Black men, which explains why Black men's marriage statistics are higher than that of the Black woman's. I'm just saying . . .

So, here is part of the problem. Most adult females are not conscious of who you are and your nature as a woman. It all has a lot to do with the way you communicate with yourself. I have some good exercises on self-communication in Chapter 6 that will help you focus on that inner voice properly. The solution to most of our problems is positive reinforcement. You'd be surprised what a little positive self-talk will do for your self-esteem.

Also, there are some things a real woman just wouldn't do, so I outlined a "Lady Code" in Chapter 18 to reinforce the ethics of a real woman. These girls out here today are just Ratchet! For those that don't know what Ratchet means, well, it's *several* steps up from a Hot Mess.

The men aren't in a much better position than the ratchet females. Many young men of this generation are the most rude, disrespectful bunch of men I've ever seen in my life! I'm not a man, but I know what a real man is. Therefore, I would

My Guide to Love & Romance

never tolerate the way these young men act if I was a young woman out here dating. This foul behavior is linked directly to a lack of Black Love, which leads to single-parent households, and when the father isn't present in any way, Mama's Boys are inadvertently molded. Then you also have this super-misogynistic genre of music called Rap. Don't get me wrong, rap music has some positive aspects, but the majority of it is very disrespectful toward women.

Many men of my generation were the most respectful men on earth. Times were different, slower, so to speak, so men knew they had to take their time if they wanted sex. It was all about respect as opposed to today. I do, however, think that some men of my generation have provided bad examples of manhood, and it has manifested in the disgusting behavior displayed by our young men today. I'm going to teach you young brothers a thing or two as well.

Young men, don't be intimidated by a strong-minded woman; understand that it is your responsibility to create that balance. Of course, a strong-minded woman is outspoken and defiant, but don't take it as an attack on your manhood. Once you dispel all the myths about women taught to you from birth and instill a positive, loving concept of women that allows you to coincide with her true nature, only then will you experience

My Guide to Love & Romance

true Love & Romance on a whole other level. Trust me when I tell you, until you embrace your woman as your EQUAL, you will never have true Love & Romance.

With all the ratchet behavior going on with both sexes, I feel safe in saying the older women and men of my generation have dropped the ball by not schooling the youth better in all areas, but particularly in the area of Love & Romance. Love of Self is the foundation to loving anyone else. When we see the youth carrying on the way they do, we can't point the finger and get angry at their behavior. IT'S OUR FAULT! It is a travesty! If older people don't step our game up and start teaching the youth how to Love each other with respect, the future is lost.

There are no rules nowadays, so Mama Jones is going to reestablish some direction up in this bitch! I'm going to address some real life shit in my guide that is long overdue.

So I'm here to restore order in the way young people perceive Love & Romance. To give it to you plain and simple, the future of this world depends on how men and women Love one another. So I'm hoping this book will serve as a beacon of Love that will shine into the future. Twenty, thirty years from now, I want this guide to be relevant.

Mama Jones
My Guide to Love & Romance

You may be asking yourself, "What qualifies Mama Jones as an expert at giving advice on Love & Romance?" Well, I'll tell you what qualifies me, and no it's not because of a college degree. It's because I'm a survivor. I have survived and came out smelling like a rose. I've been through a lot in life. It would take me several lifetimes just to tell my life story. But I would rather teach the youngsters how to Love and have a Romance with life itself.

Many times I'm asked for advice about Love & Romance, and I'm told, more often than not, that my suggestions are on the money. Hell, they should be. Three men have asked to marry me because I'm a master of Love & Romance. I've also had many interesting life experiences, from traveling around the world to living in Harlem. For me to still be alive is a miracle, so that's how I'm able to keep it real in the field, you feel me?

Listen, I've got a story to tell, and it isn't all peaches and cream. I'm going to share some of my experiences with you, in hopes that you get something great from them. When you've been here as long as I have, you know what this thing called life is all about. Trial and error is the best way to absorb a lesson, and trust me when I tell you. You can't get any better than this!

Mama Jones
My Guide to Love & Romance

You will hear many reoccurring themes in this guide; I believe repetition is good when it's something significant. When you're in school, the only way to actually absorb the lesson is through repetition. The message I'm conveying is so massive that it would take volumes of guides to cover the entire subject. Being that we don't have the time or energy for it, I'm going to cram it all in this wonderful little guide.

With that being said, you are now ready for *Mama Jones' Guide to Love & Romance*. Relax your mind and enjoy the ride.

Ciao!

PART I

COMMUNICATION

IS THE

CORNERSTONE

My Guide to Love & Romance

CHAPTER 1

"Feminine Power!

The "Pum-Pum" runs the show!"

As mothers, we have to take on many roles. You have to be a sex therapist to your man, a nurse, maid, and everything else to the kids. And you have to do all this while smiling and looking beautiful all day without breaking a sweat. My point is that I don't think women understand how powerful we really are.

My goal in this guide is to show you your power and how to use it to get a man and keep a man. That is the hardest thing for women to do. It's easy to get your nails done and get pretty, but it's not that easy to keep a man. We're going to start from point A. By the time we're at the end of this journey you'll be equipped with the knowledge to transform your life.

A lot of things that I'm going to say are pretty much common sense, but as we know, sense isn't that common anymore. You've probably heard lots of what I'm going to say before. Sometimes it's not what you say, but how you say it. Agree? You've never heard it from Mama Jones like this, so treat it like it's the first time in your life that you're getting THE REAL DEAL! Ya dig?

Let me tell you something, ladies. You can hold out on a man all you want. He'll wait; then fuck you and still dog you if you don't figure out subtle things about male/female nature. You have to appeal to his mind first. If you can't appeal to a man's mind, which is his most priceless treasure (not his DICK!), you will always find yourself as his sex slave. The ultimate way to get in his mind is by knowing more about yourself.

YOU are a reflection of your man. When you know who YOU are, you will attract the man that will reflect that. When you find him you will complement him as an equal but opposite counterpart. You become the 'Female Version' of your man by nature of being his equal opposite. So that will tell you a lot about the type of man you keep attracting. If you find yourself attracted to thugs, like many of us. Guess what? You're a fucking Thug too! You can sit there and act like a lady, but inside is a crazy bitch ready to fuck something up if she has to. Just like a thug. At the end of the day, it takes one

My Guide to Love & Romance

to know one. I just had to throw that in there because a lot of us are always talking about how we Love a thug.

See, people get it twisted; fucking and Romance are two different things. Some men think just because God blessed them with a big dick that all they have to do is run around fucking everything in a skirt and sometimes everything in pants, if you know what I mean. Men nowadays feel entitled to run around fucking everything because these young girls today are just stupid when it comes to FEMININE POWER! A woman who is independent, intelligent, attractive, and adventurous and takes control of her destiny, is a powerful woman! She uses her feminine power for the greater good and not to bring a man to his knees begging for mercy. That is a deadly form of feminine power, which is destructive in nature, unlike the kind of power I'm promoting, which is positive. We empower the world when we empower ourselves as women, because we are the mothers. Without the mother there is no family.

I figured out a powerful secret in my years on the Earth. You want to know what it is, ladies? I am a Goddess. Giving birth is an act of God. The most beautiful thing to be able to do is carry a baby inside you for nine months. As the mother, we hold life within us, and after birth we nurture. It's one of

My Guide to Love & Romance

the most powerful things a woman can do, because every birth is a miracle. Just for the sperm cell to hit the egg and for the egg to reach the first trimester is a miracle within itself.

So, what came first? The chicken or the egg? Man or woman? The Bible says the man came first, and then God took a rib from the man and made his woman. Then woman gave birth to the babies, making her the Great Mother. Who else but a Great Mother could be so compassionate and nurturing to give birth to a male child and raise him into a man?

And being the Great Mother, you know we spoil our boys and we want them to be wise and noble men. So blame the first Great Mother for the spoiling of man because that's what they are in the end, spoiled little boys. And that's how you treat them. You spoil a man and you tap into a part of him that is maternal in nature because his mother spoiled him, and she will always be his first Love. That concept goes all the way back to the first mother.

This is the FEMININE POWER that I speak about. Like I said, women have spoiled men all the way back to the first Great Mother, and that's why he now thinks he runs the world. We just let him run it while we just relax and look pretty for our Kings. It's too much work running the world anyway. Do you see all the stress men go through running things for us? Just look at President Obama, he has aged twenty years in the last four years, and he's obviously in the midst of having yet another four years of stress. But if you look at his wife, The First Lady looks like she hasn't aged a bit. In fact if you ask me, she looks more ravishing than ever. But most of all, she looks STRESS-FREE.

It's a shame young Black women today don't know or understand how much power you have at your disposal. We all have a lot to learn, right? What is better than getting some good knowledge from someone that is true?

When it's time to let your man know about your FEMININE POWER, don't hesitate. Let him know you are a Goddess. Stand firm on the principles of your newfound Love of Self to demand the respect you deserve.

Men have the tendency to treat women any old way because we let them. It's a bad habit that men have that dates back to the cavemen, probably—I don't know. What I do know is that it has to STOP! These women are your mothers, daughters, nieces, and lovers. You have to keep that in mind when you're disrespecting your woman.

I have no problem leaving a man in a New York minute. If you're not treating me the way I treat you, I'm out. It's a give and take, not a take, take, take. The problem with most women is that they hesitate to leave when a man isn't treating them right. Nine times out of ten, your man will beg to be taken back when you leave, but if you never put your foot down he will run all over you. You'll never know until you try. The worse that can happen is that he won't come back, which might be a good thing. Setting boundaries is also a part of using your FEMININE POWER. Here are a few tips:

SETTING BOUNDARIES

A. **Set a wedding date**--See how your man reacts when you mention marriage. If your man is serious about securing a future with you, he'll have no problem getting engaged and setting a wedding date.
B. **Put him on notice**--In the event that your man wants to continue to play games, put him on notice that all good things come to an end if he's not willing to do right by you.
C. **Give him an ultimatum**--After you put your man on notice and he hasn't made that move, give him the

Mama Jones
My Guide to Love & Romance

Ultimate Ultimatum—which is, if he doesn't get it together, tell him get to stepping!

When your man asks you about your new outlook on life, because your Love life will be enhanced with or without him, tell him Mama Jones told you some things that have been helpful. This is putting your FEMININE POWER to work.

Mama Jones
My Guide to Love & Romance

CHAPTER 2

"What is Love? God is Love."

Everyone is looking for Love, but the question is do they know what Love really is? This is a very generic question that usually gets a generic answer. Fortunately for you, I'm not going to give you a generic answer.

First and foremost, God is Love because His essence of Love is the reason He created the universe. Now on an earthly, human level, Love is that strong feeling you get in the pit of your stomach, usually in the form of an emotional attachment to someone or something. You can't wait to see the person all the time. You would give your life for this person.

Love is the highest level of understanding that you can have for someone or something. Being that this is a work of Love & Romance, I'm going to keep it on the topic of Love between two individuals, commonly man and woman, but not

My Guide to Love & Romance

excluding the gay community, because y'all need lessons in Love, too.

Love cannot be seen, only expressed, and one person's expression is different from the next, yet it is still all the same. Love is the only thing you can explain with words, but if you ask 100 people what Love looks like, you'll get a hundred different answers. All the responses, however, would be relatively the same. You can't give a wrong answer, unless you're into Satan worship and you say some old crazy shit. We're going to keep it basic for now. As we progress, I'll get deeper with the concepts.

To me, Love looks like my grandchildren, and the emotional attachment I have to them is so strong. It's like watching my children grow up for a second time. Love is watching my children and grandchildren be happy in life. Love is making my significant other happy. There are many faces to Love, nevertheless, Love is Love. We can only express Love the way we were taught. If you've had bad experiences with Love, then your definition is going to be much different from mine. You will probably feel miserable at the thought of Love. Don't worry, with a little understanding

My Guide to Love & Romance

you can restore the right concept of Love. That's what I'm here to do.

If you ask 100 people do they know what Love feels like? The same thing would occur; you'd get a hundred different answers that would be similar. You get what I'm saying! Love is a Universal expression of all humans, which we can all agree on no matter your religion, ethnicity, gender, or race.

A racist person can hate me because of my color, but the fact remains that he loves his wife and his children the same way I Love my children and my grandchildren. Because we all Love, it's in our nature as human beings to Love. Even a Satan worshipper loves. They may front like all they do is hate, but we know the truth. Nothing can exist without Love, that's why we use the term *'make Love'* to describe the act of sex, which is how babies are born, out of Love. Our Father God made us out of Love, and we have the power to Love unconditionally because of Him. Love is Love.

Love is very powerful. It can make you do some crazy things when you let it get out of control. Trust me, I know firsthand how Love can make you do some outlandish things. I remember one time I caught my boyfriend cheating with my best friend. I didn't yell or scream. I calmly went to the kitchen and grabbed the biggest butcher knife I could find and

My Guide to Love & Romance

I tried to stab him in his heart. Luckily for him that he was fast, so he hurried up and got the hell out of there before I could catch him.

Love is a highly emotional element that can kill. People have entered into a Love crazy trance and woke up with pieces of their mate's body parts lying in front of them. All in the name of Love. Or was it lust? Like my grandmother said, "Love isn't supposed to hurt", so when it does, is it really Love? I'm going to touch on Love versus Lust in a later chapter.

On the other hand, Love can also make you do some noble and righteous things. We all want to harness Love's essence and stay in Love land as long as we can, but Love isn't designed that way. Love's energy is so intense that often it only lasts a short time and then it's over. It is so pure that the high will take you to unimaginable heights and then drop you to come crashing down spiraling to the earth, smashed into pieces on the ground.

But Love is also a destructive force, more dangerous than the fiercest animal. It can drive a person mad with vengeance; it can make a sane person become a lunatic. Some people wish they were in Love, only to have their wish granted and then

My Guide to Love & Romance

have their hearts shattered. Be careful what you wish for. All you wanted was Love; what you got was the illusion of Love and now you're suffering from the devastating effects of being hurt. That is the nature of human Love, it can be warm and inviting one minute, cold and malicious the next, all in one neatly wrapped package.

Let me tell you something, ladies and gentlemen. Beware of the illusion of Love, which is really a delusion of grandeur. When someone really loves you there is no second guessing. If you have to ask yourself if he/she loves you, then he/she doesn't really Love you. I say this because Love can be seen through its expression. When we Love, we care and we are always showing the person through examples.

Sex isn't Love, so don't get it twisted. If a man likes to have sex with you all the time, that doesn't mean he loves you. Same thing goes for men, if a woman just likes you for your sex, she doesn't Love you.

The difference between men and women is that women tend to be more forthcoming and honest when it comes to their emotions. Men are more guarded with their feelings, so they don't express themselves well all the time. This difference creates a gap between us, because one is pulling and the other is pushing. When a woman thinks she is pulling a man closer to her by getting him to express himself, she is really pushing him away. Her intentions are sincere, but she doesn't understand his nature.

Love between a man and a woman is the most complicated because we have two different innate natures. I like to compare men to dogs. Men are like dogs because they will run around pissing and shitting everywhere in the form of fucking as many women as they can. Dogs are sloppy; they leave the evidence of their shit, just like men do. Men must know that they're dogs at heart. Why do you think they refer to their best friend as their *dog?* Just like a dog, men will hump on anything available, well any woman, that is.

But women are like cats, because like cats, women piss and shit too. A major difference between cats and dogs is that cats do their business discreetly in a litter box and then cover it up with sand. A cat's movement is graceful and sleek, similar to a woman. Women are also feminine much like the feline species, thus the term "pussycat". So we do our shit, but we just cover it up better.

Let me point out that the women in my day were like cats because of the grace in which we moved, and our sex life was discreet. We lived by the old mantra, "A lady in the streets,

My Guide to Love & Romance

but a freak in the sheets." Nowadays these women are freaks in the streets and in between the sheets. They leave nothing to the imagination of a man. That was the whole allure of holding back something and not giving it all up the first night. It makes a man go harder to please you when you make him sweat. He'll be all over you like a cheap suit.

When you give it all up to a man on the first date, you leave him with nothing to work for. Men are conquerors; they need to have things to challenge them in order to keep them interested. They get bored of women when we give it all away; then they don't want to play with you anymore. You have to keep his mind occupied with thoughts of getting what you didn't give him yet. It's a game of cat and mouse, or rather, cat and dog.

Men and women are inseparable, yet we can't stand each other every now and then. It's a phenomenon to say the least. Although we fight like cats and dogs, we can't function in a happy state of mind when we're apart. We definitely Love each other; we can't live without one another.

Love fulfills our spirit; without it, the spirit is lifeless. We need to feel the emotion of warmth and kindness, or we will wither from within. It is a fact that people that have a healthy, loving relationship tend to be more happy and healthy. When

My Guide to Love & Romance

we Love we're alive with joy and happiness, which is the goal of life—to be happy.

You may ask yourself: Why is Love so important in our lives? Besides the obvious reason of being happy, we actually need Love to fill a void of emptiness. You don't have to be in Love with someone else to fill that void, you can Love yourself to fill it. The thing is, you have to Love. We are here to Love!

What qualifies me as a chief instructor on Love? I believe in Love for everything and everybody. Not a fake Love, a genuine Love for all living things on God's green earth. I have always been a child of Love; all my friends would always come to me to get advice on Love & Romance. Over the years I have developed a heightened sense for listening to people who tell me about their relationships. I give sincere advice from the heart.

That's why I'm the way I am. I don't have time for the bull. I'll tell you like this: if a man doesn't Love me the way I Love me, then he doesn't really Love me at all. I Love myself, which is the first person you should Love after the Love of God. If you don't Love yourself, how do you expect any man or woman to Love you? When you don't Love yourself it's

My Guide to Love & Romance

easier to let someone mistreat you. Because you don't Love yourself, you allow the abuse.

Then the mystery of it all is how do we attain Love? We attain Love through Love of self. Love attracts Love. When we are positive beings, we attract Love into our lives. Because Love is a positive element, positive energy is like a magnet for Love. I know people who are so positive that they only attract positive, and I also know negative people that only attract negativity. It seems effortless for some people to achieve Love, success, and all the elements that makes us happy as humans. While others live a life of despair, never finding their true Love, and never achieving any real success

Please know that we all have a history that has shaped and molded the way we perceive Love. I've got a startling piece of news for you. In order to understand Love you have to be burned by it. Until you have gotten hurt, you don't know the other side of the coin, which means you don't have the full picture. Some of the most skilled lovers were taught by being severely hurt by the opposite sex. What I will say before I move on is that Love is what you make it.

Now that we have dealt with Love, the next chapter is about Romance. Remember that communication is the glue that holds it all together. Keep in mind that Love & Romance

My Guide to Love & Romance

are two different things that work hand in hand, but you can't have one without the other. Let's move on, shall we?

CHAPTER 3

"What is Romance? Romance is sexy!"

L ove and life. Being romantic and being passionate is the same thing.

Being romantic gives life that fire. When you Love what you do, that's the Romance of life itself. Most people that win in life have a romantic affair with their lifestyle or career, because they Love whatever it is they do. You've got to have that drive to get up and grind in life, or you will find yourself with nothing. So to be romantically involved with the grind is grinding at its finest.

I'm probably one of the most romantic people you can meet. I do things for my man that will leave his head spinning. I've been known to do some creative things in my relationship because I'm so into Romance. Later on in this guide, I will share some of the delightfully romantic things I've done that you can also do to improve your relationship.

Mama Jones
My Guide to Love & Romance

Romance is like a powerful energy that manifests itself in the emotion of Love. Romance isn't an emotion, however, it's activated through emotional energy. That's my fancy way of saying: Romance is the shit! That's how you know that you're in Love, because there is an abundance of Romance.

Romance is sexy. It's what keeps the Love alive. Without Romance, Love has no action because Romance is the expression of Love. When we say we're in Love with someone, Romance is the actual application of that professed Love. If your mate isn't expressing his/her Love with Romance, there is no Love. That's how you know that your mate loves you because he/she takes the time and energy to express the Love, not just saying it all the time. How do you know when someone loves you? The only way to know is when your mate is being romantic. We can hear "I Love you," all day every day, but if there is no action or expression, then what good is saying it all the time?

That's the beautiful thing about Romance, you can't fake it. You can only be romantic with someone you really Love because that action has to be real. You can detect when one person has more Love than the other person in a relationship. The person that is really in Love will always take the time to

My Guide to Love & Romance

implement Romance into the relationship, when the latter won't.

When a man caresses your body without rushing into sex, that's Romance. Soft lights and music playing in the background, with chocolate covered strawberries and candles is the backdrop for Romance. The rest is up to you.

Romance in Other Areas of Life

It's important to have a strong sense of Romance because it strengthens everything in your life. Like I mentioned before, Romance is the passion we have for life, not just Love. You have to be romantically involved with your career as well if it's going to be successful. We all want to be successful in Love and in life in general; those that are romantic about both are the ones that are usually happy. At the end of the day, that's what it's all about, Happiness.

Being romantically in Love is pure happiness and bliss; it gives life reason and purpose. I know for me, I cherish all those tender moments that Romance creates. Who doesn't? I mean, unless you're a nun or a priest, one of the best ways to reach the highest level of bliss is through Love & Romance.

Mama Jones
My Guide to Love & Romance

What is life if it were not for Love & Romance? As human beings we need to be loved and the Romance is what holds it all together, kind of like glue. When it becomes undone, then the fantastic voyage called a relationship is over. The Romance has burnt itself out and the Love becomes stale. When something is stale, it's like molded bread. It's time to throw it out and get a fresh new loaf of bread.

The Question Is: How Do We Attain Romance?

There is no simple answer to this question, but there is a way to achieve the highest plane of Romance. Always remember that Love & Romance is a state of mind that can be altered. You have to be in the mindset to be romantic, or it won't work. If your thoughts are on work or a future football game, then achieving Romance is futile. You have to be there in that space to even want to be romantic. Some people think they're being romantic, but in reality they're not. Romance isn't sex, it's looking into your lover's eyes and touching their face, kissing their lips softly. Romance is very silent, you don't have to speak to be romantic.

My Guide to Love & Romance

In fact, the best Romance is unspoken and more mental telepathy than anything. Remember, in order to achieve supreme Romance, first you have to be in Love. For example, when your man looks you in the eyes, then he gently kisses your lips and rubs his groin against your vagina. You know it's about to go down, there is nothing to say; just let the Romance flow. You learn to let Romance move in its own rhythm, or you'll destroy the moment.

Most of the time it's the little things that create the biggest effect on a person when it comes to Romance. For example, if I'm in the shower and my man comes in and washes my back for me, or we're just laughing while having pillow talk. It's the subtle things that mean the most. Romance doesn't have to be expensive, just being there and spending time is all the Romance you need sometimes. At times, just showing your partner that you care is a romantic gesture that costs you nothing. I Love to spoil my man. I make sure all the little things he needs is there, like his razor and aftershave lotion. I like to make sure my man is well groomed. I Love to cook for my man. I think that is one of the most romantic things a woman can do for her man. It's very sexy and romantic for a woman to take the time out to cook a good meal for her man. Let me tell you something about the romantic connection you

My Guide to Love & Romance

achieve by cooking a good tasting meal for your man, ladies. There is more going on than meets the eye. Eating is spiritual; it's sustenance for the mind, body, and the soul. There is the subtle concept of caring, and being thoughtful when a woman cooks for her man. It is true that a way to a man's heart is through his stomach.

There is nothing more sexy and romantic than when a man knows how to cook. Cooking is not just a woman's sport anymore. More men are getting into the culinary arts. Just look at all the cooking shows, and you'll see them looking masculine in their aprons. It increases the Romance whenever your mate cooks for you, but when it's the man, it just does something more for a woman. I guess it's because it's usually the woman in the kitchen. It dispels the myth that it's a woman's job to be in the kitchen cooking and cleaning all the time. It gives us that much deserved break, which allows us to really appreciate the Romance of the whole process.

I like to show my true feelings through my actions. Romance is Love at the end of the day, because it's the Romance that created the Love. Although they are two different things altogether, one can't exist without the other. If you tried to separate the two, there wouldn't be a solid

My Guide to Love & Romance

foundation to nourish a relationship. Everything needs nourishment, even a relationship. Romance becomes the sustenance for Love in the relationship.

It's like a rose garden; when you see all the roses start blooming you appreciate the beauty of the garden. That's like Romance, when you feel the Love you start to appreciate your partner and the beauty of the relationship. Romance is the end result of being in Love, just like the actual rose is the end result of the seed. The seeds of Romance must be watered in order to see the manifestation of it.

Romance is very short-lived, one minute it's thriving and the next it's dying. Just like most things that make us feel good, it doesn't last long. Those of us that have mastered the art of Love & Romance understand that it takes great energy to keep it alive. It is a combination of wisdom, patience, and a few other virtues that I'm going to outline for you. Here are a few suggestions on how to keep Romance alive.

KEEPING ROMANCE ALIVE

A. Be original when thinking of ways to be romantic.
B. Create adventure, there's nothing more romantic than adventure.

My Guide to Love & Romance

C. Surprise your significant other often, become the master of surprise.

D. Don't do the same things over and over.

E. Take advice from successful relationships.

These are just a few things to keep in mind when trying to keep Romance alive. None of this will work if the communication isn't there. I'm going to get into how important it is to open up your mouth and speak, or forever hold your peace.

CHAPTER 4

"A Closed Mouth Don't Get Fed
Learn how to speak directly from the heart."

P art one is all about COMMUNICATION. How can women and men communicate efficiently when we have a double standard? It's impossible for a male chauvinist to have a serious conversation with a woman when he thinks of her as just a lay. It's cool for a man to have many women, but if a woman does the same with men, then she's automatically a whore. What's good for the goose is good for the gander, so men are the biggest whores! Let's face it; there are more 'hos today than ever in history. Because of the double standard, women probably feel that now they can have their cake and eat it too. Women have grown tired of that old cliché about being a slut or whatever. They want to date different men just as men date several women. What happened was that women began to enjoy it a little too much, and it has gotten out of control.

Mama Jones
My Guide to Love & Romance

This chapter is all about the importance of speaking out, because when you don't open your mouth to speak, how will you be heard?

Communication is truly the cornerstone of any relationship. Without communication how do you get to know someone? Unless you're using mental telepathy, speaking, not talking (talking is a low form of communication), is the only way to make that connection. When you speak to someone, there is a process of paying extreme attention with respect. You know when you're interested in something or someone. You listen closely and speak concisely, and nine times out of ten there will be a connection.

Now, what do I mean by *A closed mouth don't get fed*? Usually this term is used in the streets to mean if you don't open up your mouth to speak about yourself and what you're doing, no one will know. Pimps and hustlers have to have the gift of gab in order to get money on the streets. Even for aspiring artists that are trying to get out there, if no one knows about you and your talent, it's useless. But if you are out there meeting and talking to people about what you do and your talent, they're going to know about it. If you're good you will

My Guide to Love & Romance

get money, which we call EATING. Just by speaking to people, you have fed yourself and your whole family.

When my son first started his solo career, he had to promote himself. If he didn't constantly talk about what he was doing, he wouldn't be eating. Jelmoe (Jim) started out with Cam'ron, better known as Cam, who is a rapper and actor. Cam and Jelmoe were childhood friends. Cam got signed to a record label and brought Jelmoe along for the ride. Jelmoe used to handle management roles, and he even shot videos for Cam. He was instrumental in helping Cam's career. The whole time he was assisting with Cam's career, Jelmoe was recording his own album.

I used to listen to my son's music and I really liked it, and not just because he's my son. I remember telling Jelmoe, "Now that you have helped Cam'ron with his career, it's time to get your career off the ground."

Jelmoe went out there and single-handedly built his solo career from scratch. He was out there beating the pavement, scheduling meetings, and he landed his first record deal. In 2006 I was still living in Harlem. I remember Jelmoe came into my room and lay beside me and said, "This is all because of you, Mommy." He showed me a check for $175,000. "If you wouldn't have encouraged me to go hard with my solo career, I wouldn't have this check in my hand."

I cried like a baby. Memories. It seems just like yesterday. My son's career is similar to a relationship because just like a career, a relationship requires a lot of work. As it goes with a career, you have to Love what you do, or you will dread that job and leave it. You have to be in Love with the very idea of being in a relationship, or you will never have a successful relationship. Same goes for a successful career.

In the context of Love & Romance, the term *"a closed mouth don't get fed"* means if you don't open up and speak honestly about yourself, then how do you expect someone to be open and honest with you. It is a give and take, but if you don't give then you don't receive. You may be scared to open up because of what happened in the past, but never let past experiences ruin your emotional energy. Just because someone chooses to be foul, that doesn't mean you have to be foul. Open up your mouth and speak freely from the heart, with honesty, and you will receive the same as you give. Your plate will have an abundance of Love & Romance that will fill you up.

Mama Jones
My Guide to Love & Romance

You have to know how to communicate, which brings me to the issue at hand. Most people don't know how to communicate properly, and that's why they're always misunderstanding things. They aren't completely honest, and they don't speak freely from the heart. When you fake it to make it, eventually the true you surfaces and then you look as phony as a three-dollar bill. That's not a good look. All you wanted to do was impress someone. Not only didn't you impress them, but now they think of you as a lame.

Never fear, Mama Jones is here. There is always a good solution to any problem. The problem of communication can easily be solved with the proper instructions. That's the wonderful thing about life! You get chances to change things about your life that you don't like or that aren't up to par. With a little information and the right application, anyone can transform into a better person. You just have to be willing to embrace knowledge and you will get insight.

A closed mind is worse than a closed mouth, because when your mind is closed you cut yourself off from getting new knowledge. If you can't receive new information then you will remain on a base level of life, not growing and developing into a better person. We all have to be able to learn new things in life or suffer from being mediocre. There is nothing worse than a person who is content with being average in life; we should all want to improve standards in our lives. That is why you're reading this guide, because you're a person who's open to new ideas, so here we are.

I am a people person, so it's easy for me to communicate with others in an embracing manner. You don't have to be a people person to communicate well, but you have to Love self and everyone else, or you won't even have the desire to communicate well with others. I am a true believer in the power of communication. I believe that if we as a human species were to learn to communicate with one another properly, this would be a perfect world. Racism would self-destruct because when we communicate we have a better understanding of one another, dispelling the lies and myths about each other. This simple concept alone will create that Oneness that the world is missing.

I'm going to outline three steps to a better style of communication. I'm not saying that these steps are going to make you have an intelligent conversation. It's a basic foundation to keep in mind when you're trying to have a great conversation.

Step 1. **Learn to speak directly from the heart.**

Mama Jones
My Guide to Love & Romance

When you learn to speak directly from the heart, you will come across genuinely as opposed to fake and scripted. In a relationship, it's very important to be not only honest, but brutally honest. Even if you think what you're about to say will be hurtful, say it anyway if it's from the heart, and don't be mean-spirited when you say it. I recall having to speak the truth to my man and watching him almost cry because what I said was too real. Afterward, he thanked me for being honest, and it enhanced our relationship, instead of destroying it.

Step 2. **Take your time and think about how you feel.**

This step should really be first, but I made it second because once you make the choice to be honest and speak from the heart, then you take your time to think about how you feel before you speak. When you take a deep breath and clear your mind, you'll notice that your speech will parallel your thoughts. Sometimes we tend to jump the gun when we want to get our point across to our partner; we speak from an emotional space. Whenever emotions are involved, things can get misconstrued. How you feel at that moment is based on that emotion, which will pass and you may regret what you said. Never speak to your partner when you're emotional. Wait until you are relaxed and calm, then take your time and think about what you're going to say. That is the best way to communicate efficiently.

Step 3. **Choose your words wisely.**

Your choice of words is very important. A whole message can get lost in translation by speaking the wrong words. After you've made the conscious decision to be honest and speak from the heart and you've taken a deep breath, cleared your mind and balanced your emotions, choose your words wisely. Most people are not very good at communicating, so they will always choose the wrong words. However, with patience and practice, anyone can learn to communicate effectively. Even if your vocabulary isn't vast, when you follow these three easy steps, you will notice that communication with your partner will be easy and comfortable. Once you both practice these steps, I can guarantee a loving and happy relationship.

Contemplate on these steps before using them. Understand what each one means so that you may be efficient at communicating. You will find that comfort zone with your mate that seems impossible to achieve. There will be no more mistrust, insecurities, or questioning the loyalty and Love of your mate once you learn to communicate properly. Nothing happens overnight, however, with time and patience you will become the master communicator. Your conversations become persuasive and almost hypnotic. I remember this one man I was dealing with used to have such great communication skills that I would sit and listen to him for hours without interruption. I actually started to fall hard for this man, but I had to let him go because he was too much of a player. He had my mind with his intelligence, but I saw through his game, and you know Mama Jones don't play no games. I'm a grown ass woman!

Learn how to communicate and then open up your mouth. You never know, your soul mate could be right around the corner waiting on you to speak. You'll know when to use the skills that Mama Jones just taught you. Keep in mind that everyone has their own self-styled way of speaking; make sure yours is smooth for that extra added effect.

Good luck on your journey through Love land.

My Guide to Love & Romance

CHAPTER 5

"Talk is Cheap; Action is priceless!
Bring sand to the beach and the living room too!"

T he worse thing a man or woman can do in a relationship is talk a good game that is recognized as a game. You know the braggadocios, the conceited people of society that think they're God's gift to the world. Please! I just want to smack fire out of these types of people! We all know someone like this; the world is full of them, especially in America. America is the breeding ground for these types of people. After all, we are the richest nation on the earth.

This particular group of people is always talking, mostly about themselves. You will rarely find these types in an intelligent conversation. Their ego is so big that when you pop it, you have just killed a part of them because their self-image is largely based on his or her big ego. These types can be very annoying! They aren't aware of their anti-seductive behavior,

My Guide to Love & Romance

so they carry on as if everything is cool, when in fact it isn't. It will practically take a life-altering experience for them to realize they have to come back down to earth.

These types are mainly financially successful, or beautiful on the outside, but ugly on the inside, and they are always in some drama. Does this sound like anyone you know? Chances are you know someone like this. Everyone does. The world is filled with mindless people who are motivated by drama and nonsense. Drama is what fuels the ignorant. When I meet someone I can automatically tell if they're a drama Queen or King. When I determine that you're one, I'll cut you off in the snap of a finger! I'll say it again, Mama Jones don't play!

The Difference between Talking and Speaking

Remember when I said, talking is a low form of communication? That's because a person is saying something with no significance. When someone *speaks* it's about something with substance, and believe me when I tell you, every woman loves a man that can hold an intelligent conversation. That is the difference between speaking and talking. Like they used to say, "Anything after but, is bullshit."

Men often say too much when they're trying to charm a female. Let me tell you guys something, less is more. Always say less than necessary, you never know when you just shot yourself in the foot by saying something stupid. If you can't hold an intelligent conversation, learn how to have one. Read books to strengthen your vocabulary and read the newspaper to stay up on current events, surf the Internet, so you'll have important things to discuss. Surround yourself with people that are highly intelligent and learn from them. You'll notice the change in the way you think and act, which in turn will give you the skill and confidence to hold an intelligent convo.

I've met some very interesting men in my day, and I've met some lame ass dudes. The men that were interesting to me were always the silent, strong types that knew exactly what to say and what not to say. These men were intriguing and mysterious; they knew how to communicate without speaking sometimes. Body language and eye contact are a very intricate part of communication as well.

When you find that mate skilled at communicating without being verbal, you have found that rare jewel. They are out there. You just have to dig deep to find them, just like mining gold and rare gems. Sometimes you meet a good brother with close friends that are just like him. So when your girlfriends ask you if he has a friend because you speak so highly of him you can say, "He just happens to have a good friend that is just like him." It's always a grand occasion when there are more people to celebrate life with. Particularly when you are all like-minded, that's what creates the atmosphere for Love & Romance to magically happen. Good friends, good food, some drinks and music in a dimly lit lounge, and watch as the night of enchantment unfolds.

I've always liked to play matchmaker with my friends. I've been able to arrange a few meetings that turned into life-long partnerships. I know what type of woman to introduce to a certain type of man. You know what I'm saying? You can't hook up two people that aren't compatible. Then you'll be the one they'll blame when things go sour. When shit was sweet, you were the savior of the day, but let things go wrong. Then they'll hold you responsible for the day they ever laid eyes on one another.

Now that we have established the difference between talking and speaking, let's look at how actions are omnipotent and beneficial to developing great communication skills. I

My Guide to Love & Romance

spoke about the strong silent type. Well, they're the shining example of actions speaking louder than words. When your heart is in the right place, your actions become significant and they have more meaning than any word you could utter. This is communication at its finest.

Your actions can create the most loving environment, something words cannot do. Words can actually limit a loving experience because words can be interpreted in different ways. One sentence can be interpreted by me in one way, but when you hear the same sentence, you get an entirely different meaning from it. But actions can never be interpreted differently by anyone because actions are pure and are less likely to be misinterpreted. For example, when a man buys a woman flowers, he doesn't have to say one word. The gesture itself speaks volumes. We can safely assume that this man was thinking about her, that he is considerate and cares about her feelings, etc. I can go on for days.

This is one simple action. There are deeper, more complex actions that can make a person fall so deep in Love that it creates a heavenly experience of Love & Romance. I can't tell you how to work your mojo; every situation is unique. I know that when you think long and hard about how to do anything, there is a moment where you have an epiphany. You come up

My Guide to Love & Romance

with the perfect way to show and prove your Love through your actions. You eventually become good at being creative at displaying romantic actions. You can't lose, fellows, if you pay attention to what Mama Jones is kicking. Your woman will stay so deeply in Love with you, that you couldn't pay her a million dollars to leave you. The mere thought will give her stomach pains. I'm telling you! This is some good shit, top of the line game, baby!

Ways to Surprise Your Man

I can't teach anyone how to act, but what I can do is give you the wisdom that can show you a thing or two. I'm no expert at teaching, but what I am good at is giving people a piece of my mind on any topic. And my opinions on this topic are concrete. When I tell you that actions can work magic on your mate, trust me, you have no idea!

A few years ago, I wanted to do something different for my man on Valentine's Day. I did just about every romantic thing that I could think of for this man. "What can I do that will excite him that I haven't already done?" I thought long and hard about it, and then I came up with this brilliant idea. It was

My Guide to Love & Romance

relatively cold on Valentine's Day this particular year, and being that I'm originally from Aruba where it's tropical all year round, I wanted to bring the Caribbean to my house. Why not change my living room into a beachfront? I called my sister and told her my idea, and she helped me make it a reality. I mean, we brought in the sand, palm trees, the background of ocean and blue sky, with beachfront chairs. When I was finished, my living room looked just like my own little Aruba.

When my man came home and saw a tropical heaven right in the living room, he was speechless. His mind couldn't comprehend what was going on. He had never seen anything like this before in all of his years. "No woman has ever done anything like this for me," said my very surprised man.

There is no amount of money that could pay for the genuine reaction my man had. The expression on his face was priceless! When you learn the art of communicating through your actions as well as words, you can create a long-lasting loving affect that you desire in a relationship. Don't get it twisted; speaking is the best way to communicate if you're a novice. Take it from me, doing something creative trumps saying words all day.

My Guide to Love & Romance

Nonverbal Communication

There are many ways to speak loudly without shouting verbally. One of the most common ways is with body language. For the ladies, it's a slight touch on a man's shoulder or his hand. It is a subtle way of letting him know you're interested. You don't always have to throw yourself at a man to get his interest. Sometimes it's better to be discreet. A man with class will appreciate the subtle nature of your advancement. That's the way you preserve more to the imagination. There is electricity in the touch of a hand that is supernatural. It connects you to an etheric-like energy that is highly spiritual. When the Love is deep and the Romance is at its apex is when the human touch becomes a conduit to a blissful experience. Human touch is very formidable to say the least.

When you're not able to be nonverbal, most likely you're the type that seeks attention. Wanting attention isn't a bad thing, it's human nature to want some form of attention to feel like you're not invisible. Some people, however, become extreme with seeking attention. These types can often resort to drastic measures for the thrill of being admired by everyone in

My Guide to Love & Romance

their presence. Which leads me to my next magnificent term that I like to call the *'THIRST-BUCKET'*.

Thirst-Buckets

Now I must take the time to address the actions of women that I like to call *Thirst-Buckets*. I have to get at you because this chapter is about actions, good and bad. Here are some of the things that *Thirst-Buckets* do. I'm out there with my son, and I see all you thirsty-ass bitches always flinging yourselves at him. I've seen women so thirsty and desperate to get at my son that they will do it in front of his girlfriend, Chrissy. It's these type of women that give us all a bad look.

Let me tell you *Thirst-Buckets* something. No real man is going to pick up some trash in the street to wife up, especially when you do it like that. I'm telling you the truth. Have some dignity, ladies. You don't have to act this way. Learn to at least mask some of the thirst. I mean, damn. I've never seen this many *Thirst-Buckets* in my entire life. It has to be an army of these types of people.

Ladies, when you're on your A-game with your swag— your hair is done fly, nails and toes are done, your outfit is smashing, and you smell good, you don't have to throw

My Guide to Love & Romance

yourself at a man, he'll come to you. Nothing gets a man's attention more than a well put together, beautiful woman with swag. After you have all that in check, walk with class and hold your head high. You will have the appearance of a person with quality and the aura of a goddess. Now all you have to do is strut your stuff and watch all the men flock to you. It is all in the way you carry yourself.

And for the fellows, shouting "Yo, ma!" or "Shorty, let me holla at you!" is getting a bit played out. I get the whole thug fascination, but some of you guys are just down-right disrespectful! Your mother should have taught you better than that. You get exactly the type of ratchet female you deserve, because no real woman will deal with that type of behavior. I told myself when I started this book that I didn't want to male-bash, but I have to call a spade a spade. It is what it is. That doesn't mean someone shouldn't address it. That's the problem nowadays; no one wants to keep it 100 % real, until it's too late. Then they want to point their fingers like, "Look at how these guys act." Well, tell them to stop acting in that manner, and why it's beneficial for him to take heed to your advice. It's not what you say, it's how you say it.

Mama Jones
My Guide to Love & Romance

Fellows, if you want to impress a woman, all you have to do is stand out from the rest of the pack. Women will see you as intriguing because you look different from all the other males, and they will instantly become interested. You don't have to be loud and obnoxious by saying things to get women to notice you. Believe me when I tell you, as soon as you walked your corny ass through the door every woman in the spot noticed you, so save the variety act. All you have to figure out is how to do things that are abstract, and you will receive attention from all types of exotic women.

Women love to be surprised and excited. When you are an adventurist, it arouses a woman to the point of no return! Trust me when I tell you, once you've figured this out there is no stopping you from getting any woman you desire. Just don't blow your cool and it'll be smooth sailing. Update yourself on your swag and keep on keeping on, young player.

Just like I prescribed for the ladies, men, you have to stay fly, or as they call it nowadays in the hood—flee! There is nothing on earth more attractive than a man that has his shit together. I mean from head to toe, with a mind and the right body language and it's a rap! That's the man that can have his choice of women every time he steps into public. He's not the loud mouth always bragging about what he has, and name-

My Guide to Love & Romance

dropping everywhere he goes. He's the quiet, conservative man that has the eminence of royalty. He lets his swag speak for itself.

When you've mastered speaking to communicate, then practice letting your actions do the speaking. You'll see the big difference between the two immediately. Actions last longer than words because you will remember a loving action forever, as opposed to something sweet that someone said to you. Thus, the saying: "Actions speak louder than words." We can all agree that it is better to be a person that shows and proves with actions, than to be a good talker that gets nothing accomplished.

So, who is the best person to communicate with? Yourself, of course. The way you communicate with yourself makes the difference in how you communicate with others, and ultimately life itself. Before we move on to the next chapter, I'll leave you with a question to ponder: How can you become a person whose actions parallel who you say you are?

CHAPTER 6

"Self-Communication is Important
If you don't Love yourself, how are you going to
Love someone else?"

The way you communicate with yourself is one of the most important things to establish. Let's see if you were paying attention. Remember what I said in the beginning? Essentially, I said that in order to Love someone, you must first Love YOU. Most people don't realize that listening to that inner voice and speaking back to it in a healthy manner is how we develop a sense of Self and who we really are.

We're not just what you see on the outside. There is an energy that is animating the body. Much like a car, there has to be someone in it in order for the car to move. Well, the body is just a vehicle. There is a force or energy inside operating the vehicle, that's the inner voice I'm speaking on.

My Guide to Love & Romance

The ever-present Self, the pair of eyes looking back at you when you look at yourself in the mirror. Next time you look in the mirror, look very closely and you can see the Self staring right back at you. And I'm not talking about the reflection either. Figure that one out.

Most people haven't learned the basics about communicating with the Self because it was designed that way. *"The Powers That Be"* wouldn't be in control if the masses were to wake up to the reality of the Self. Knowledge is power. They are able to stay in Power by withholding true knowledge from the masses, and keeping them in a state of illusion. If everyone understood this concept, then the world would be a well-adjusted society, and Lord knows it's not.

Learning to Trust in and Listen to Your Inner Voice

Now what do I mean by Self-Communication? Self-Communication is the messages that you tell yourself about yourself. It is that inner voice of God speaking to you. God is always present, and believe it or not, He warns you and tells you when to go hard, and when to stop and regroup. That intuition that tells you, "Don't go out tonight. Something is going to happen." And the next day you hear about people

My Guide to Love & Romance

getting shot and you would've been there if you wouldn't have listened to that voice. Then you say, "Something told me not to go to the club last night." Or when that inner voice tells a woman, "Something about him is very creepy!" Come to find out he's a rapist and that mental suggestion just saved your life. If that's not communication, then I don't know what is.

We all speak to ourselves, and what we tell ourselves dictates our view of ourselves and the world. How we view our Self is so important to maintaining a comfortable state of existence. For instance, a woman that sends a message to herself that "I'm fat and ugly; I'll never find a man that wants me" is destroying her self-image and creating insecurities at the same time. This will result in depression and a myriad of other mental issues. It is a fact that the way you think and communicate with yourself has a profound effect on your self-image and how others will perceive you.

The masses are blind to this fact. It is like magic to see people transcend the perception of what society says is beautiful. Like the overweight woman that says to herself over and over, "So what I'm fat; I still look good." Or to see a man that isn't physically attractive at all, but there is something about him that attracts the most beautiful women on earth. It is

My Guide to Love & Romance

all about how you communicate with yourself. How you see yourself is ultimately how others will see you. It is that simple.

Let me explain something to you. Whenever a negative thought about yourself enters your mind. Kill it as fast as it was born. It is very important that you understand this concept because these thoughts are like cancer; they spread and grow into serious life problems. If anyone says anything negative to you or about you, never internalize it because you will ruminate, and it will destroy you from the inside out. I've seen people wither away, literally, because of repeated statements of negativity. Just look at these kids that are committing suicide because of others bullying them at school or on the Internet. It's becoming an epidemic. Words have the power to encourage greatness, or they can lead someone to misery, or even worse, suicide.

Also, run far and fast from those that judge and spread rumors because it will consume you and you will become like that person. They only judge because they dislike their lives, so their thoughts are negative. Your thoughts become your reality. Eventually, life mirrors your thoughts. Then these negative-thinking people wonder why their lives are filled with all kinds of drama. We all know a person or a few people that are always into drama. **WARNING**: if you keep them as

My Guide to Love & Romance

company you might become just like them. Negative thoughts are worse than cancer because chemo can't shrink this kind of tumor. The only way to cure your mind from negativity is to communicate with yourself correctly.

Practice being positive at all times. You will witness a transformation taking place on the inside. Your quality of life will increase ten-fold. Colors become brighter, everything seems light, and nothing is heavy enough to weigh you down. Negative people will try to pull you down from your new high, but you won't let them because you've figured out the secret. Life is really what you make it! You're finally living life on life's terms.

We are taught not to talk to ourselves because only crazy people do that. You communicate with yourself whether you want to or not, because the mind is always wondering and seeking balance and truth, so it is always communicating on a sub-conscious level. God is the truth. I'm telling you because if it were not for his amazing grace, we wouldn't have a sound mind to have free will to think and to communicate the way we do as humans. It is a direct gift from the Most High God that we are blessed with the ability to communicate on many different levels.

My Guide to Love & Romance

That's why humans are the only species on earth that have the ability to speak intellectually. Show me any animal on earth that can do that. There aren't any. As smart as dogs, dolphins, cats, and monkeys are, they will never hold an intelligent conversation with you. An animal might be able to make sounds that communicate, or a few words, but never in the history of my living have I ever witnessed any animal that can speak fluently. Humans were blessed with great creative and academic skills that come straight from our Father, who art in Heaven. Thank you Jesus! God is good. God is great!

Now that we have established the fact that Self-communication is a powerful tool when it's understood, let me give you some exercises that will help you to communicate with yourself better.

Step 1. Repeat positive messages to yourself daily.

When you repeat a positive message daily, it's called Positive Reinforcement. Positive Reinforcements are like wheels you create in your mind. Once you say them the first time, your mind creates the wheel. When you repeat them the wheels start turning. When the wheels start turning, the message materializes as a peaceful balanced inner feeling. When you get up in the morning, look in the mirror and say,

My Guide to Love & Romance

"I'm a beautiful, talented, and caring human being, and I'm going to have a great day." Start off with this statement, but as you advance you can make up your own Positive Reinforcements. Once you've mastered the concept, you can make up different reinforcements for different problems in your life. For instance, let's say you're having relationship problems. You can create a Positive affirmation custom-made to that particular situation. This step is for all the state of affairs in your life.

Step 2. Destroy any negative thought on sight!

I spoke about this earlier, but I have to reiterate it because it's a very important step. Just like Positive Reinforcements, you can create Negative Reinforcements as well. When you allow the seeds of negative thoughts to be planted in the garden of your mind, then you water them by contemplating on them. They will grow like weeds, killing anything good in the mind's garden. It's a very easy practice, all you have to do is repeat a positive reinforcement and you kill the negative thought instantly. Make sure you destroy any negative thought on sight; it will be the difference between happiness and sorrow. It is all in the mind.

My Guide to Love & Romance

Step 3. Maintain your new positive attitude and enjoy life.

This step is self-explanatory; once you've mastered the first two steps, all you have to do is maintain your newfound positive attitude toward life. All the problems of your life are all in your head; trust me when I tell you that there is someone doing worse than you.

And when it comes to Love & Romance, a positive attitude will make you appear to be the most loving, caring person that exists. Why? Because that's what you'll become. God wants all of his children to be happy and in Love. He created everything out of Love. Love is the cause and the effect of everything in the Universe, so it's always the answer to any confusion.

This will conclude Part I on Communication. When I say Communication is the Cornerstone, I sincerely mean it. Communication is the key to understanding, and understanding is the goal when you want to really know someone. Yes, you can know someone on a basic level, like their name and where they're from, etc., but do you understand the person? Like I've pointed out, if you don't know how to communicate properly, you'll never find the true

My Guide to Love & Romance

Love you seek. When I say communicate properly, I don't only mean with others, but most importantly with yourself. When you master how to communicate with yourself and others, you don't have to look for Love. True Love will find you.

Remember to repeat the three steps I laid out for better self-communication.

Step 1. Repeat positive messages to yourself daily.

Step 2. Destroy any negative thought on sight!

Step 3. Maintain your new positive attitude and enjoy life.

Prepare your mind for part two. Oh yeah, I have a few jewels to drop on you that will improve your existence. I'm not perfect, but I still have a bit of wisdom to drop on you. We're going to move on to my favorite section of this whole book—Keeping it real! Are you ready? Then let's go!

PART II

Keep it Real

at

All Times!

CHAPTER 7

"Self-confidence is Paramount!
It's very important to think highly of yourself"

P art two is all about KEEPING IT REAL! I specialize
in keeping it real, it's all I know. I don't know any
other way. The world has become so shallow that it
seems that being fake is in style. I just laugh to myself when I
hear all the fake shit that goes on in the world. I don't know
what has happened to all the people that used to keep it real.
There used to be more realness back in the day. I'm truly the
last of a dying breed.

What do I mean when I say KEEP IT REAL AT ALL
TIMES? I mean exactly what I Say! You see, when you're as
real as me, it comes natural. In our natural state of mind we're
as real as they come. When you add the pressures of society,
you get a manufactured reality, which is fake. Everything is

My Guide to Love & Romance

based on materialism, and how much money you have in the bank. In times like the one we are living in, you need someone to step up to be the example of Real. However, most of the world has to be taught how to keep it real, so that's what I'm going to teach in this chapter.

Keeping it real starts with Self-confidence. When you are secure with yourself, you don't have to be fake. When a person is self-confident, they don't have to front or perpetrate a fraud. They are so confident in the Self that it's senseless to be something else. I learned a long time ago that confidence in yourself is attractive. When you exude that confidence, people flock to you, and they view you as an important person, without knowing why.

Every real player will tell you they got their game from a woman. Where do you think Jelmoe (that's my nickname for Jimmy) got his game from? I taught Jelmoe everything he knows about the proper way to treat a woman. Not to brag, but my son is real SMOOTH with the ladies, ya dig!

I taught all my children to have high self-esteem and self-confidence. It definitely helped them to have a balanced social life. They were all popular in school and they did positive things in the community. Well, Jelmoe got caught up in selling

My Guide to Love & Romance

drugs for a short period. In fact, all the kids in Harlem were victims of a dirty trick the Government was found guilty of, but that's another story.

My son is just like his mother because he radiates confidence; sometimes it can be mistaken as conceit. Jelmoe is so confident that he attracts success to himself. A person that is self-confident has the air of being highly important, someone who is goal-oriented and relentless in their pursuit of success. Show me a successful person and I bet he or she is self-confident.

I'm going to keep it on the topic of Love & Romance, but the principal of being self-confident extends into career goals as well. When dealing with Love & Romance, Self-confidence is a paramount element. When both people in the relationship have self-confidence, there is less bickering and more understanding. These type of couples tend to stay together for decades without a break-up. There is a balance between the two that creates a loving and romantic atmosphere.

However, there is such a thing as being over-confident, which is anti-seductive behavior and can push people away. When a man or woman is over-confident it creates an atmosphere of animosity and hostility. Over-confidence comes across like arrogance, and people will see it and not like you for it. Arrogance often leaves a bad taste in a person's mouth that will last as long as they know you. It's very true what they say: The first impression is a lasting impression.

If you don't learn anything from this guide, you have to know that a person who isn't confident will not attract Love or Romance into their lives. I've known physically attractive women that lacked confidence, and they were always in dysfunctional relationships, or just single. I don't care how pretty you are. Ladies, if you don't have self-confidence, men will detect it and capitalize from it. They will take advantage of your weakness, because that's what it is. It's a real jungle out there. The strong are those with conviction and certainty. The weak lack assertion and self-reliance and suffer from mediocrity. I didn't make the rules; that's just how the world works. Yet, I don't agree with it. If I had it my way, things would be much different.

And fellows, it's even worse when *you* don't have self-confidence because you're just lame. That's right, I said it! A man is not officially a man if he is not confident, because your manhood is in the balance. Part of being a man is being confident in your ability to be a man. Women will pick up on it immediately, and most likely, a strong-minded woman wouldn't be interested in a man that lacks confidence. Most gold-diggers seek out rich men with no confidence because they're easy to control.

How do you know if you lack self-confidence? Is there some type of meter that can measure our confidence? Self-confidence can only be expressed, much like Love & Romance. Too much confidence and you are anti-seductive, too little confidence will make you seem corny. You've got to have just the right amount to pull off the job.

Well, here are three questions that will determine if you lack confidence. Don't think hard about the answers. Say the first answer that pops into your mind spontaneously. Answer them honestly; this is between you and yourself, so it's 100% confidential.

1. When you look in the mirror do you like what you see?
2. When you think of accomplishing a goal, do you second guess your ability to achieve it?
3. When you see an attractive person does the thought of being with them intimidate you?
4. Well, if you answered No, Yes, Yes, then you probably lack self-confidence. If you answered Yes, No, No, then you're safe.

My Guide to Love & Romance

5. If you're not confident in yourself, here are some tips that may help you gain some self-confidence. Although the following is only my advice, it can still be life-changing depending on your mental level.

6. Understand that God created you as a perfect being. Even the crooked tooth was designed that way by God, so in that case it's perfect. Know that you're a unique individual; there is no one like you, which makes you one of a kind.

7. Beauty is in the eye of the beholder. You are the beholder, so embrace your own beauty. Understand that everything God creates is beautiful, inside and out. Embrace your beauty.

8. Find that Happiness inside that will give you the confidence that you lack. There is a space inside of every being that is happy, confident, secure, and free from negative thinking. When you find it, stay there for a while and then learn how to go there at will.

You will see your life transform. Just like the caterpillar morphs into a beautiful butterfly, you will gain the confidence to do whatever your heart desires.

Mama Jones
My Guide to Love & Romance

Take it from Mama Jones, God Loves all of his children, and He wants us all to be happy with our existence, for it is a gift from God. It is a blessing to be able to see, hear, walk, hell, even to talk (which is something I Love to do). People are always complaining about not having money, or not having a good job. I'm here to say: Shut up and stop complaining! Don't you know there are people that can't put their own pants on, people that can't talk, see, or hear? Those people have a lot to complain about, and most of them don't. Believe me, they know what I'm speaking about because they have to find that happy space, or they will drive themselves nutty. We can't even imagine what they have to go through. I commend all disabled men and women out there for being resilient in the face of adversity.

You want to know what people do when they can't create their own happiness? They constantly try to find it in other people, or things, like drugs. If you can't be happy on your own, most likely you won't be happy with another person. No one wants to be with an unhappy person, because an unhappy person is a miserable person. Misery can contort your physical body into something ugly, and health issues can also occur. That's right! You can contract an illness from being miserable. I've been around a long time, and I've seen it with my own eyes. Health is a state of mind altered from case to case. Studies have found that patients given placeboes recovered faster than some patients that were given actual medication. The patients given placeboes healed themselves, because it's all in the mind. Humans have incredible self-healing abilities.

So if you have a negative state of mind, the vibration will make you more susceptible to feeling sick. It may be all in the mind. Nevertheless, the sickness becomes real. Knowing this bit of info is very pertinent to maintaining your health. Avoid negative thinking on any level. It can actually save your life.

Have you ever seen a miserable, negative person? Seriously, just look at them. You can see the misery and the negativity manifest in them physically. That's why miserable people are always single, because no one wants to be with a miserable person except another miserable person. That doesn't last, because eventually they'll get tired of each other's misery. In the end, a miserable motherfucker is, well, just a miserable motherfucker!

If you're looking for Love or Romance, avoid misery at all costs. Even if you're not looking for Love & Romance, and you're just looking for happiness and success, find that space and be what you were meant to be, a beautiful child of God. I

My Guide to Love & Romance

know it's hard to be happy when your bills are due and everything seems to be going wrong. Trust me, those are just tests to see if you're worthy of His blessings. Remain steadfast, and you will weather the storm. It gets greater, later.

You might ask yourself, "Why is Mama Jones always bringing God into it?" Because God is Love, and without God there is no Love. He created everything out of Love, and that Love gave birth to the whole Universe. So we can't talk about Love without bringing God into the equation. GOD=LOVE!

So what did we learn? I'll tell you something, confidence can save your life. I hope you take heed to my words on self-confidence. When I was a young woman, I used to hang out on the streets of Harlem with the hustlers, players, and pimps. Back then the streets were very cold as they are today; the only difference now is the times, and the fact that some of the values have changed. There were rules and regulations in the streets, things that you knew you weren't supposed to do. Not like these days where you can violate the rules and there is no penalty.

If it wasn't for the confidence that my mother instilled in me, I would've been so naïve and the wolves would've eaten me alive. Because I was head-strong, it was hard for the hustlers to take advantage of me. They had no choice but to

My Guide to Love & Romance

respect me because I demanded it. I saw how they would treat females who lacked the confidence that I had, so it made me stick to my guns even harder. No man has been able to break my confidence; I've been that way since I was a little girl. My mother used to tell me, "Your man is going to have a hard time with you, because you're no pushover."

That's right. I'm not a joke when it comes to someone showing me my proper respect. However, I am very considerate and respectful to everyone. I believe that people with self-confidence are the same way. It's a matter of treating others how you'd like to be treated, simple as that. If more people had self-confidence, the world would be a more pleasant place. It would limit hating and increase the Love. Don't you want to live in a world where people Love instead of hate? I do, and that's why I'm personally making an effort to change the way we Love. I know that having this discussion about Love & Romance is the key to a better way of life for all of humanity. Stay with me, this ride is about to get crazy.

CHAPTER 8

"No Love Without Romance!
Money can't buy love; it can buy
The illusion of romance."

Everyone is looking for Love. Some find it in themselves, and others try to find it in someone else. First of all, if you haven't found it in yourself, you're looking in all the wrong places, as the popular country song goes. We've already established that Love of Self is the best Love of all, because in order to attract the opposite sex you must first Love Self and be confident in the Love of yourself. What about Romance? Can you have Romance without Love of Self? The answer is yes and no, depending on the individual. I know it's a contradiction, but nevertheless, it's true. Stay with me on this one because it can get complicated.

Let's analyze this closely. Yes, you can create the illusion of Romance without having Love of Self if you have a lot of

My Guide to Love & Romance

money. Men and women alike, can actually buy romance by doing all kinds of expensive things for their significant other. There are a lot of rich people who are so miserable they become severely depressed. You would think that having lots of money would make anyone happy, but you're wrong. Love and Happiness has nothing to do with money or riches. Don't get it twisted, money can't buy Love. What it can buy is the illusion of romance.

What do I mean by, "Money can buy the illusion of Romance?" It sounds self-explanatory, but it isn't. You see, without Love of Self, Confidence, and great Communication skills, the person with money is feeding a negative monster that will show itself eventually. The monster was born from a lack of confidence and the wrong messages being communicated to the mind. Because of the way society dictates that money is power, the person with money is lured into a false sense of reality. Money isn't power, because I know men without a lot of money who control things, and they're very powerful because they have a lot of knowledge. And I know lames that just happen to have money but can't command respect. The man with a powerful presence stands like a giant amongst lames with money.

Mama Jones
My Guide to Love & Romance

When I was young I dated this man, not because I liked him, but because he kept throwing money at me. I barely paid him the time of day, yet he kept showering me with gifts thinking he would get some poom-poom. I never liked him, and he started to notice it and he became violent, so I had to cut him off. I guess he thought just because he had money I was supposed to fall in Love with him. Fellows, let me tell you something. It doesn't matter how much money you have, if you lack the things I've spoken on, then a woman will only use you for your precious money. When the money is gone, so is the woman. The Love & Romance was superficial.

I know it sounds harsh, nevertheless, that is the reality of the world we live in today. You can be a wise man, and a good person at heart, but that will get you but so far if you're not getting money.

On the other hand, there are always exceptions to every rule. I've seen broke guys who lacked self–esteem win chicks over by just being very kind. To a damaged woman, even a lame with no money can look like Superman. I've seen men and women get lucky and bag a good catch because of circumstances like a death, or a bad break-up, which leaves one vulnerable. God allows worse things to happen, so an odd

My Guide to Love & Romance

couple is just one of those acts of divine intervention that happen in Love Land from time to time.

Love & Romance are intertwined; you can't have one without the other. When couples that have been together for years start to fall out of Love, it's because the Romance is gone. Romance is the fabric that keeps the Love intact, or what keeps you *'In Love'*. You can Love someone very deeply, but when the Romance is gone the Love becomes platonic. The Love loses its depth. You're no longer falling in Love; you're falling out of Love.

For those of us that have been through it, you know the feeling when you're falling out of Love. You're no longer attracted to the person anymore; their presence starts to annoy you. It's almost like a death because you know the Love is gone, and when it's gone there's no coming back. It's always one person in the relationship who has more Love for the other person.

It's that person who is usually the most damaged. They want to try things to rekindle the flame, but prolonging it only makes it worse. Sometimes you have to learn to just let go.

In order to know Love you must experience the heartbreak and pain of it. You can't know Love until you've been to the

My Guide to Love & Romance

other side, because when things are all peachy and sweet, you can't fathom things any other way. You get complacent in the relationship and can't imagine that this person who claims to Love you, has just hurt you badly. When things get sour, you're blindsided because the deep emotions can drown you.

If you're in Love it's because the Romance is always present. There is always that challenge to out-do yourself when thinking about how to please your mate. You get butterflies just thinking of pleasing your mate, to the point that you could orgasm (only if you're a woman). It's the most beautiful feeling to have both Love & Romance. It's what created man, woman, and child and the entire Universe. Remember, "God so loved the world that he gave his only begotten son . . ." Now that's what you call Love. Even if you're not Christian, you can grasp that statement.

I have to keep stating how important it is for us to Love. A person without Love isn't living life because it is Love that makes life's experiences enjoyable. It is the Love that gives us that fulfillment from living. And to be romantically in Love is one of the most beautiful achievements we can aspire to. It is truly a heavenly experience. I speak from experience.

What would Love be without Romance? I don't think it would be Love at all. That's what you call lust. Now, you

My Guide to Love & Romance

could be in lust with someone. Being in lust requires no Romance whatsoever. You just have to agree that the relationship is strictly about sex, and the business of lust can take place. It has no depth, no spiritual meaning, and it's short-lived. Lust is considered a sin, which it is, yet it has to exist in order to understand Love.

We've all been in one of those situations where you're sexually attracted to someone, but that's it. Some of those relationships can be very steamy and give the appearance of Romance, but it's not Romance. It's just good old fashioned lust. When one of you catches feelings and you want to take it to the next level, then there's a problem. The lust can disappear in the blink of an eye, because it was created out of something that had no depth. Lust is finite; it has a beginning and an ending, whereas Love is infinite. When we learn the true characteristics of Love, it becomes easy to separate it from lust and fake Romance.

There is one simple way to avoid bullshit in Love land and in life in general: Keep it real at all times! Life is too short to be faking it. That's why some of you are always getting played in these relationships; you're not keeping it real! That's why there is no Love or Romance, and most likely no success.

Mama Jones
My Guide to Love & Romance

When you bullshit your way through life, that is exactly what you get—BULLSHIT! One day it will dawn on you that life is too short to be playing around. One day you'll wake up and see that you've wasted precious time.

You see, this book is about more than just Love & Romance it's about Success & Happiness as well. It took me almost half of my life to figure out some of the intricate details about Love. I catch myself saying, "Wow, it's that simple." Most complex things in life are very simple in nature. It's all about coming to the realization of God in your life and how he has been blessing you from the start. My life became balanced once I realized that God Almighty allowed me to wake up with good health through all the hardships I've survived. He blessed me with the insight to be able to speak to you in this way. These are not my words; they are His words. I'm just a vessel relaying the message. When we let go and let God, Love & Romance flows effortlessly into our lives. Along with it will come everything that your heart desires.

CHAPTER 9

"You Can't Rush Love!
Wait at least six months or a year before having sex.
Beware of Academy Award winners!"

I f you made it this far in my guide, this section begins
Part II, which is all about keeping it real, which is what I
do best (I'm just saying). Once you've mastered all the
steps I've given you on great communication and self-
confidence and you're ready to find true Love & Romance, it
may take months, even years before you find your true Love.

You have to understand, the world is filled with derelicts
that prey on weak-minded people for self-gratification. So you
have to weed through the sea of losers to find that special one,
because by now you're confident and you know your value, so
you're not going to settle. For instance, let's just say you meet
a guy that is so handsome he makes your vagina flutter (now
that's what I call handsome.). He has all the right stuff,
intelligence, humor, vision, but he has a woman. He claims the

relationship is on the outs. Do you still take a chance to be with him?

Emphatically No! If you have learned anything from this guide it should be patience. Taking the time to find the right guy is important. You can't rush Love, so in this case you'll tell homeboy he's qualified for the position, but not right now. You value yourself more than anything, and you know that you're worth the wait. Try again in six months or a year. But me personally I like the year.

Let me tell you something, when I divorced my second husband it took me almost eight years before I was ready to settle down again. There were a few times I thought I would settle down, but the signs were telling me that I was rushing it. I didn't want to rush into a relationship and go through the whole process of him meeting my kids, and we don't work out. That can mess with your kids too, because they get attached easily. I wanted to be single for a while, so I could regroup and get my mind right.

Relationships can take a huge toll on your life. The energy it takes to maintain a relationship is overwhelming. The same applies when going through a break-up, which usually lasts up to a year. No one just breaks up, it's a process. So that means

My Guide to Love & Romance

that you were in a failed relationship trying to find a way out after you realized it's not going to work. The problem with that is, it takes a while to figure out that it's not mendable. The romantic in you keeps trying to fix it, but once it's broken, it can't be fixed sometimes. It all depends on the severity of the offenses.

I'm going to give you a remedy to figuring out a person quickly. I know this from living in a fast paced place like Harlem. You have to pay attention to every detail. See, most of you just pay attention to flashy things and materialistic stuff. When you pay attention to every word and action, you will figure things out that are important. The objective in a relationship, especially in the beginning is to see if this person is genuine enough to give yourself to.

This is a special message to some of you good people that are reading this book right now; you don't need to rush into another relationship. Some of you (you know who you are), need to be alone for a while to get your life balanced just to experience it, for the growth of it. Just look at the stars, they break up and are on to the next before they've given themselves time to heal. Most people hate being alone. Every human being on Earth needs to be in the company of other

My Guide to Love & Romance

human beings; it's our nature. But we don't need other people to validate who we are.

On the contrary, the masses think they need someone's approval to feel important. When you learn to feel very important because you understand that God made you that way, then you don't need anyone to provide that feeling. There are a lot of benefits to being alone, one of them is Self-Realization. When you isolate yourself you will have epiphanies about yourself and life in general that you might not have had otherwise. You're left to deal with you and only you, so all the issues start to get dealt with. Once you come to the realization of self, your perfect match will appear. Remember, the goal is to find that perfect match that completes your life. I mean, let's be real; life is more enjoyable when you're experiencing it with someone you Love.

You can have this life-changing moment where you understand Love, but how many others have come to this realization? Trust me, not many. So take your time finding that person. He or she is out there waiting on you to mysteriously appear into their lives. Most meaningful relationships happen very subtly and naturally. It's when

My Guide to Love & Romance

you're not looking for something, is when it finds you. When you get all dressed up to go to the club looking for that special person, you find the opposite, which is a person that appears to be the ONE, but isn't. It can take months or years sometimes before you figure out the person is a FRAUD.

I'm going to keep it real with you. There are some very clever and cunning individuals out there that should win Academy Awards for the roles they play. You could be with someone for seven years and think you know them, but you don't know them. You only know who they pretend to be, a made-up persona. They could be playing you the whole time. That's why this chapter is all about taking your time when you're looking for true Love & Romance. There is no rush when it comes to finding Love. That's why I recommend that you be single and let it happen when it's supposed to.

Some of you think it's okay to have a booty call in between relationships, and I'm saying that you don't need that either. I'm actually advising that you be celibate until you find your true Love. I know it's hard not to have sex, but trust Mama Jones when I say that sometimes sex can hurt you more than it helps. Obviously, some of you can't separate sex from Love. Some people can't just have casual sex without getting emotionally attached.

My Guide to Love & Romance

For people that have had multiple failed attempts at a happy relationship, I recommend you go on a sex-fast. Even when you think you've met that special person; don't have sex for at least a year. I know it sounds crazy, but that's the best way to connect with someone spiritually and emotionally. The sex is physical, and can have a negative side-effect sometimes. I'm going to put this into steps because it's very important.

SEXUAL FAST

A. Remove all forms of sex from your life for at least six months to a year.

B. If you meet a man during your sex fast, do not break it for him.

C. During your fast, focus on your spiritual energy.

D. Live your life as normal as you can although a sexual fast is unusual.

The Downside of Having Sex for Women

You might ask, "What is the negative side-effect to having sex?" Some men, but mostly women, suffer from what I like to call 'Sex Attachment Syndrome' (SAS). SAS is a fancy

My Guide to Love & Romance

pants way of saying, "You are pussy whipped or dick whipped!" depending on the gender. You get it. Some people fall in Love with the sex, which is a dangerous situation because it can make you do crazy things. One of my close friends suffers from SAS. She cannot have sex with a man without getting extremely attached. Especially if it's good, then you can forget about it. She'll be looking for that dick in the daytime with a flashlight!

That's why I highly recommend that you take your time, and really get to know the person well before you have sex with them. If he/she really values you, then he/she will wait as long as you want them to. You'll experience the difference when you wait, because the sex will be explosive! You will swear on a stack of Bibles that it was the best sex you ever had in your life! Most likely it was the best sex because you allowed yourself time to let the mental do the connecting first instead of the physical.

Always remember, sex is all in the mind. When your mind is stable and you've found that space, you will have the most loving and romantic experience of your lifetime. It is the mind that regulates our sexual encounters and determines the level of the climax. Your mate must be on the same plane, or you

My Guide to Love & Romance

won't have the best experience. It'll just be good. But sex with someone on your level is absolutely divine.

So, what have we learned in this chapter? Most of the things I've written seem to be self-explanatory, but they're not. Know when it's time to Love. Just because you get lonely doesn't mean that you should rush to be in a relationship, especially when you're damaged. I always suggest that every woman go on a sexual fast every now and then just to tune-up and strengthen your focus. Give yourself time to heal and don't look for Love. You'll be surprised, because Love will find you once you've found yourself.

Here are a few suggestions I'd like to share with you on finding yourself:

☐ Keep a journal—Sitting down to think and write about the events of the day is very therapeutic. It helps you point out things that you would've done different to make better future decisions.

☐ Meditating—I know I've said this one before, but I can't stress it enough. Meditating relieves tension and clears the mind to help you find that positive space you need to be happy and successful.

My Guide to Love & Romance

☐ Prayer—Prayer and meditating are one and the same, but different altogether. Prayer is your connection between you and God, while mediating is the connection between you and the Universe. God gives you answers in the form of blessings.

CHAPTER 10

"Be Original
Originality makes us unique."

Originality is what makes us unique. I can tell you that originality is something that the world is lacking. I see so much of the same that it's ridiculous. Everyone is looking and talking the same. Hell, people are even acting the same. The world is void of flavor, something we had an abundance of back in my day.

Part of keeping it real is being authentic and most of all, original. I have to state this because there's nothing like a person that takes the time to be really spontaneous, quick-witted, and ready for adventure. The beautiful thing about life is that we have so many wonderful ideas that the possibilities are endless. When I turned my living room into a beachfront to surprise my man, it was an on the spot idea. Once I made that idea a reality, it enhanced so many things in my relationship. One of the first things that came to my man's mind was how original my surprise was. He marveled at the

My Guide to Love & Romance

fact that my mind had even come up with such an original plan to surprise him.

When you are original in your ideas of Romance, the Romance is always taking on a new form, which keeps everything in the relationship in tune. It is like living a virtual heaven on earth, to continually have a spark in your relationship. I know from experience, or I wouldn't attempt to write this book. When my manager came to me with the idea of writing a book, I had to think about it for a minute. I have to be real about whatever I do, so I thought of it as a way to express myself in a medium other than reality TV or songs. I found the book process to be more informative as I went along. I'm far from done, but my point is that the book idea was original for me because prior to being on *Love & Hip Hop*, I had no interest in the limelight. It's one of those things that chose me; I didn't choose it. However, I'm very grateful to God for giving me the opportunity. All the things I've done in the last five years have been original in the aspect of it being new to me. My life has been this never ending adventure that keeps exhilarating me beyond belief. My life has never been boring, but now it's just incredible! Praise God!

Mama Jones
My Guide to Love & Romance

My goal is to share my life experiences with the masses so they too can have this incredible feeling that I'm having. I wish my whole life was like this, but unfortunately for me it wasn't. I have had many downs before I came up, lost many battles but I won the war! Now I live to make sure that my children and my grandchildren experience life as an adventure too, and not as a grudge match for survival. God did not intend for us to live life unhappy, or without Love & Romance. I realized this late in my life.

Now I just want to spread the word so I can inform as many people as possible before it's my time to go. I've never had this feeling until I started writing this book. It has been very therapeutic for me to write this work, because it has given me great purpose. We all need to have purpose in life; it's what makes life worth living. And that's keeping it 100 percent.

Being original is a major component of keeping it real. God is always original in his plans, because he is the best of planners. When we embrace the concept of always being original in everything that we do, every day is filled with the prospect of a new start. We are forever evolving and changing our mindset. Whether we realize it or not, our spirit is always being original. The spirit is the origin of human Love; it's the conduit for positive change. It is the human spirit that motivates us to be in Love.

I know that my son's originality is one of the main elements of his success. Growing up in Harlem, you had to be original. Anyone who has ever been to or lived in Harlem knows that we take pride in being the first to do something, especially fashion. There is a mentality in Harlem to be extremely original. You don't get noticed when you look and act like everyone else, but when you're original everyone wants to know what you're wearing or what you're doing.

For the fellows this is very important. A woman will get very bored if she sees you're not original; it means you're not real and you're a follower. She will drop you for the guy that is always being original in his approach to Love & Romance. For instance, the guy that brings flowers and candy for Valentine's Day isn't being original. The guy that has the flowers delivered to her job with a singing telegraph declaring his Love will win as an original idea, even if the idea has been thought of before. It's still a more exciting gesture than just flowers.

My point is that originality trumps tradition. Think outside the box. Do things that will make you seem larger than life.

My Guide to Love & Romance

Now you are exciting the essence of her being, which is her mind. Once you capture a person's mind, you have won the game of Love. The mere thought of you brings a smile for minutes at a time. That's a lot of damn smiling!

It's hard for this generation to keep it real with all the fake influences being heavily promoted to them. I'm sincere when I say that I'm dedicated to restoring some type of order in the way the youth perceive things. Their views are so distorted that when I think of our future I get worried. I hope that a large number of young people are able to read this book. I think it will help our society because the children are the future. If they don't have balance then we are headed for chaos. I have grandchildren that I want to live in a sane world when they get older. You can't even go to the movies without fear of being killed by a crazy person because society is so fucked up. Imagine how it will be ten, twenty years from now? It scares you, doesn't it? It should.

As long as Mama Jones has breath in her body, I will spread God's message of Love for all mankind. I will not go down without a fight, and I have God with me, so I pity the fool that tries to stand in my way. We all need to realize that we are all one. Only then will we change the world right here and now. Not tomorrow—TODAY!

With that being said, this concludes Part II on keeping it real.

PART III

Make Time for

Love!

CHAPTER 11

"Work Hard; Play Harder!
Make time for Love, regardless of
how much you work."

W ith the economy at an all-time low, people are forced to work two and three jobs. There is not enough money or time to spend with the family. It is a very difficult situation, but you have to make it work, or live a life of despair. In the end, though, Love will prevail; it never fails.

I've always been an advocate of playing hard. My son Jelmoe is just like me. He party's hard, but he also works hard. You can't play hard without money, and money comes from hard work. Life is no fun if you can't play. When you're in Love there has to be playtime. That's part of the Romance. If I could, I would go out every night of the week. For some time, after *Love & Hip Hop*, I toured the country doing appearances and performing "Psychotic". For those who haven't followed the reality show *Love & Hip Hop*, my son's fiancée and I don't get along. So on one of the episodes she called me 'psychotic'. I took that insult and recorded a song called "Psychotic".

That was the time of my life, every night in a different city getting paid just to be in VIP. Most people don't know that many reality TV stars make a lot of money by doing VIP appearances in clubs across America. I see what Jelmoe has to go through with the groupies and the haters when he's out on tour. They go hand in hand. You learn to Love them all, even the haters. But this train is fueled by Love and the Grace of God, so all you haters stop hating and embrace Mama Jones' message of Love. That's if there are any hater's reading this, which I hope not, but anyway . . .

Hard work allows us the opportunity to play hard, which results in that feeling of success. When you have a career that is successful, you have to Love what you do in order to call it a success. The idea of work excites you and gives you great meaning and purpose. You can't hate what you do and call yourself successful. When you hate your job (whether it's eight hours or more) you subject yourself to live in misery. It doesn't go together, one cancels out the other in a game of opposites. So, is Love success? Not really, but then again it is.

Mama Jones
My Guide to Love & Romance

It's kind of a paradox because Love isn't success, but to be in Love is a degree of success. We all yearn to be loved, and when we are in Love we're very happy. That is success within itself. One person's success is another person's failure, so the measurement is not standard. It is all based on the individual's perception.

Success has nothing to do with money. On the contrary, being spiritually connected is more successful than having lots of money. Some millionaires are what I like to call *spiritually bankrupt*. Their souls are empty because with every dollar they made, a piece of their spirit was torn from the soul. That happens when people make lots of money from stealing or getting rich by poisoning the population like some corporations do without a conscious. Nevertheless, I digress. I'm not going to chew your ear off about my definition of Love and success. There's a lot more to discuss.

Like I mentioned before, if you're original and creative, you can make $100 look like you've spent hundreds. My point is that when you're in a relationship you always have to think on this level, because the minute you start to slip—there goes the Romance.

My Guide to Love & Romance

That's the funny thing about Romance; it fades so easily, because in essence, Romance is generated from pure thoughts. It is all about your state of mind that creates Romance; if your mind isn't in the right place you will never attain Love or Romance. Romance is kind of like the child of Love, because Love is always the foundation, and it nurtures Romance. We can agree that there is definitely no Romance without Love.

I often contemplate the significance of Romance. I came to the conclusion that Romance is essential in any relationship. I've been in situations where there was no Romance whatsoever, but there was great sex. After the sex was over, I couldn't wait to get away from the person because there was no Romance. On the other hand, when there was Romance involved, I wanted to cuddle and snuggle up with my man after a session of hot steamy sex.

As humans, we long to be in the company of our loved one, and our family. That is some of the best memories you'll have, when you're happy spending time and having fun with your mate. We need to have those special moments in time to fulfill the soul. Playing hard and having fun is the ultimate way to achieve a sense of wholeness with the Self and the Universe. If you haven't been there to that inner place, this guide will show you the way.

My Guide to Love & Romance

The main point of this chapter is to get you to understand that working hard to play hard is a great way to sustain a happy, loving environment. Having fun in life is what makes life worth living, because having fun makes us happy inside. When we have fun playing and laughing we get a sense of extreme bliss. I mean, who wants to live a life of despair without Love & Romance? These are the things that fulfill that inner space where all the good things reside.

Like I said, I play harder than I work because at my age hard work isn't too popular. I like to let loose, free from scrutiny. I've been blessed to be in a position that I'm in today, mainly because I have a positive spirit. However, I believe that my success is due to my playful nature, because I'm just a kid at heart. Of course, I'm a responsible adult, but having a child-like nature is what keeps a person young in more ways than one. People are always asking me what my secret to looking young is. I tell them, you have to be young at heart first. Just like children play, adults play, although our fun is more mature, it's all the same. The playful nature of the child is why they seem young, because they have lots of playful energy. That playful energy is what will keep you looking young and healthy. It will also keep you light on your feet, because you don't sweat the small things in life.

When we work hard at anything there is a feeling of reward. Have you ever had a hard day's work and you walk away feeling a sense of accomplishment? That feeling is the spirit responding to the exertion of positive energy. For example, when you have an intense workout, your muscles are sore from the energy you just used to sculpt your physique. Well, that is what happens with our spirit, it relishes in the glory of the self when you work hard. Hard work is sustenance for the soul.

At the end of the day, working hard and playing harder will manifest that balance you need to create the environment for real Love to materialize. The atmosphere has to be right for Love to happen. You know how they say the stars must've been aligned when Love happened. Well, you have to be in the right space and time for something deep like Love to happen. There's nothing like a fun place filled with positive people, which is where you go to find Love. The vibe has to be right, and playing hard automatically creates it.

Here are some tips on balancing a relationship with hard work:

Mama Jones
My Guide to Love & Romance

1. Make sure you add a date night to your already busy schedule.

2. No matter what, do not make excuses not to make it to date night. Make it a priority.

3. Communicate with your employer about your relationship. When you request time off to be with your significant other they'll be more understanding.

4. Plan a date night that includes other couples.

5. On date nights try to do something different every time. You don't want things to get boring.

These are just a few tips that aren't written in stone. You can add on to any of my tips, I urge you to. That means you are participating, and participation leads to perfection, eventually.

We're going to tackle one of my favorite topics in the next chapter, Lust. I can't wait to get into it. What am I waiting for then. Let's go

Mama Jones
My Guide to Love & Romance

CHAPTER 12

"Love Versus Lust

Occasionally let lust in behind closed doors."

All this talk about Love got me to thinking about Lust. You do realize that you've got to have Lust involved with your Love life? Lust is the erotic twin sister of Love. Lust is a nasty slut. She gets it in when it comes to fucking, not making Love—just good old fashioned FUCKING!

Ladies, let me tell you something. If you don't let lust into your relationship then your sex life will suffer severely. Same thing goes for men. If you don't let that lust rise up every now and then, you'll never experience great sex. You have to get down and dirty sometimes. It's fun to go there occasionally. I'm not saying that you have to let lust in every time you make Love, but I'll explain why you MUST let it in every once and a while.

Mama Jones
My Guide to Love & Romance

This is an old secret that a lot of young folks don't know about. Some of you older veterans reading this already know what I'm talking about. I'm not advocating that we should Lust openly. I'm saying in the bedroom behind closed doors you have to introduce Lust into the equation. When I say let Lust in, be very careful because things can get crazy if you don't regulate it. I've heard of some bizarre stories about people getting out of control with Lust. You have to understand that sexual energy is what propels a relationship when it's done right. That's why sex is a big part of a relationship. It is the way we express our Love & Romance. Without sex in the equation, how would we know intimacy?

We understand that Lust is one of the seven sins, but that doesn't exclude it from being a part of sex. Now I'm a devoted Christian, but there is no way that I'm only having sex to procreate. What about just having sex for the sheer pleasure? For the emotional bonding that it provides in a relationship? I have enough wisdom to determine that God doesn't judge us for being human.

So what am I saying? It's simple. You can be attracted to someone, but it doesn't mean that there is going to be Romance involved. We are creatures of habit, so we often do

My Guide to Love & Romance

things out of a need, and not a want. My girlfriends are always saying, "I need some dick."

You don't need any dick, because you're not going to die if you don't get it. You want dick, and if you're attracted to the person, he's going to get him some pussy, and if the dick is good, a sista might just fall in Love. Remember, no one falls on purpose, that's why most of the time we don't know who we are going to end up with.

Most women have a button connected to their concept of Love. What I mean is, the majority of women get some good dick and fall in Love. Their clit is connected to their heart, so sex becomes a powerful tool when a woman is desperate for Love. The same goes for a number of men. Some men have tender dicks, so any pussy will get them open. As humans we have an overpowering need to be loved. It's definitely not just a want, attaining Love is a need.

Will you die without Love? This is an interesting question, because I've heard of cases where newborns died because they didn't get enough human contact. Newborns need to be held and nurtured, or they can die. Does this apply to adults? Strangely enough, it's true that as adults we can die inside, but not a physical death. It's only an emotional one. I've known people that went twenty years without a mate, and those individuals were rigid and suffered from severe loneliness.

Now, there is a wrong way to Lust. When a man is gawking at you and making lewd comments, that is a problem. Some men can't help it. They Lust so much that it's like second nature. A woman will walk pass, and they can't contain the urge to turn around to see her ass. I raised a male, so I know all about how men are firsthand. Some men are borderline psychopaths when it comes to Lust. That's what makes men rape women; they take lusting past the limit.

Lust is the equal opposite of Love. Everything that exists has an equal opposite. Meaning, where there is an up there is an equal and opposite down. You can have one without the other, but they are often interdependent. In situations where there is deep Love, at the core there is always a subtle hint of Lust. When a man watches his woman sashay across the bedroom in panties and a bra and he's thinking, "Damn, that ass is nice. I want to just bend her over the bathroom sink and fuck the shit out of her, right now." And then he actually does it with passion, that's controlled Lust. No one got hurt and both parties had a great time. Lust is like a nasty way to desire someone.

Mama Jones
My Guide to Love & Romance

Now, let me share a little something with you about my concept of Love. Most people believe that when you're in Love, you can only be in Love with one person at a time. Well, if you ask Mama Jones, "Can you be in Love with only one person at a time?" I'll say that you can Love more than one person at a time. That's right! Mama Jones said it. I believe in loving more than one person. I believe in polygamy.

I know most people can't fathom this, but for me it's the truth. Kanye West said it best in his song "Church in the Wild" when he said, "Love is cursed by monogamy." I couldn't have said it better myself. Love is so big. How can it just be between two people? Just think about it for a second. Have you ever wanted to be in Love with more than one person? Maybe I think too much like a man, but I understand why men do what they do. It is possible that you can Love more than one person.

Now can you be 'in Love' with more than one person? That's another question that creates controversy. I'm not sure about this one, because to be 'in Love' takes a lot of energy, so being 'in Love' with multiple people would take up too much time and energy. I guess it's possible, but I wouldn't attempt to be 'in Love' with more than one man. Loving someone and being 'in Love' with someone is two different

My Guide to Love & Romance

things. Being 'in Love' is the extreme end of Love itself; it's the height of Love. So to that one I'll say no, you can't be 'in Love' with more than one person, but you can Love more than one person intimately.

I have five children with three men. Jelmoe and his sister Precious have the same father. His name was Armando, but we called him Mundy. Mundy was the Love of my life, and the only man I will always Love no matter what. Mundy was what I like to call the most 'beautifully strange' man that I ever met. He touched me so much. I really miss him. He passed away in 2001 right before Father's Day.

Then I have two children, Alcua and Alexis with their father, Luther. And last but not least, I have a daughter named Khadija with her father Keith. I loved all of these men. I made some mistakes in my life, but having my beautiful children wasn't one of them. I Love all of my children the same. Just like I Love all their fathers the same.

Then my third marriage was to a man named Beany. Beany was my Junior High School sweetheart. He was a real bad ass, but he always treated me like a lady. Beany and I were like Bonnie & Clyde (partners in crime). Beany was my knight in shining armor. We're separated for now because he says VH1

My Guide to Love & Romance

destroyed our marriage. When *Love & Hip Hop* started getting big, I became very popular, so I had to be out all the time taping and doing appearances. So Beany and I agreed to separate. What was I supposed to do? Turn down all that money, not Mama Jones. I'm about my paper. He'll be back, trust me on that one.

I know most people won't agree with my concept, and that's okay. I'm not trying to force my views on anyone; I'm just merely stating how I see things, being that this is my book. I'm a little eccentric when it comes to Love & Romance. I came to understand that about me—everyone's not going to see things like me. That's what makes us all unique.

We all want to be in a relationship that is full of Love & Romance; the only problem is that Love & Romance are difficult elements to achieve. If it were easy to attain Love & Romance, then this world would be perfect. I say that because Love is the only thing that can bring the masses together, being that we are all divided proves that Love is hard to achieve. People have to learn to Love. It's not as simple as it seems. If anyone reading this book is in Love, hold on to it as long as you can because it's the most precious emotion we can grasp. It is a task trying to keep Love alive, and it takes a lot of

My Guide to Love & Romance

hard work. Anyone that has been in Love can attest to what I'm saying. Lust is an easy sensation to reach, but Love isn't that easy to accomplish.

When you find your true Love you'll know it. You'll feel it in the pit of your stomach; you won't be able to get the person off your mind. If you have ever experienced true Love and lost it, that's okay. There's an old saying: "It is better to have loved and lost than to have never loved at all." Make sure that you're not mistaking Lust for Love, because it's very easy to get the two mixed up.

If your mate is only concerned with having sex with you, he is probably not in Love with you, it's just Lust. If he isn't interested in taking you to dinner, or if he hasn't taken you to meet his mother, he's probably not in Love with you. Most men take a female to meet their mother for two reasons. One is to get Mother's approval, and two is to let her meet the woman that birthed him. It's very important that your man takes you to see his mother. It means that he's serious about you and this isn't just Lust, its Love.

My advice to anyone seeking true Love is to be genuine and never chase Love because it will run far and fast from you. Take it from me, Love hates to be chased. Lust, on the

My Guide to Love & Romance

other hand, likes to be chased and caught. When it is all said and done, Love and Lust go hand in hand, but Love is the foundation. The foundation has to be solid for the House of Love to be strong. When the foundation is solid, then the actual House of Love will stand the test of time.

Understand the difference between Love and Lust. Make sure you know what you want. If you just want Lust out of a relationship, be sure to be adamant about your intentions. Some people really don't want to be in a relationship. They just want the Lust of it—just the sex, which is cool, as long as you are honest about it. Remember, in Love land you have to be brutally honest, not just for the sake of it, but to protect your feelings.

And if you want Love out of it, make sure your partner wants the same thing, or risk being hurt. There is nothing that will cause you more grief than to be in a one-sided relationship. The person that is in Love versus the person that is in Lust is a situation that eventually cancels itself out. The person who's in Love will ultimately demand equal respect, which is difficult for the person that is just in Lust.

Know for sure what you want in a relationship. Speak honestly from the heart and let the chips fall where they may. Just keep in mind that you can only tell a person what you expect, you can't force Love. Letting go is the best thing to do at times. As much as it may hurt, sometimes you have to walk away and try again. I will tell anyone, you don't want to waste your life trying to be happy. Learn to be happy! Trust me, there is someone out there for you, just waiting for you to appear with all your Love & Romance.

CHAPTER 13

"Timing is Everything! Time is of the essence;
it determines the exact moment when you will meet
that special someone."

T ime is of the essence, it determines the exact moment when you meet someone that potentially may be your life long mate. The date and the time of a seemingly chance meeting are very important. That's why we measure our relationships by anniversaries, because the date you met is a very important one. It becomes almost as important as Christmas is, as far as holidays are concerned.

Ecclesiastes 3:1: To everything there is a season. Often the time or season just isn't right for Love or Romance to occur. Oranges don't grow in the winter because it's not the proper season, that's the same for Love. Have you ever met someone you were really attracted to, but for some reason the timing wasn't right? I have, and let me tell you something, I think about the person every now and then because it never worked out. I was in transition from one relationship, but he wasn't, so he wanted to move a little fast. I wasn't feeling the same way because the timing wasn't right. If it would've been at least three months between my break up, then it would've been better for me.

Sometimes priorities conflict with timing. A lot of professional people suffer from timing in a relationship. When you're working all the time and your mate is longing to spend time with you, it can get complicated. Feelings get twisted, and the Love starts to fade. As it fades, it drives you further from the goal which is that wonderful union.

Trust me, I know from experience. When *Love & Hip Hop* aired, we never thought it would be that big. I thought it would be a good show and everything, but it got more ratings than VH1 anticipated. Then all of a sudden the requests started coming in, it was crazy. Promoters from all over the country requested that I come through to perform "Psychotic", or just to post up in VIP for a couple thousand dollars. I didn't have time to get a decent rest, let alone be home laying up with my husband. And just like I said earlier, the Love started fading.

Timing is everything; it can be the difference between that everlasting Love that you seek and no Love at all. When the

My Guide to Love & Romance

timing is right you'll know it because things will just fall into place naturally. You'll have everything in common, and most likely you are both recovering from a bad break. Everything will seem like a coincidence, but it's not. You were destined to find your true Love at exactly the right time and not a second before.

Being in Love can feed positive energy into your spirit, or it can take a huge toll on your spirit when things go sour. When you've been in a long loving relationship that didn't work out, it takes something from you; it's like a death. It's very disappointing, because you invested all of your time and emotions into nurturing something you would give your life to protect. You start to feel unappreciated and used when a man doesn't appreciate you.

Women become hopelessly attached in a relationship because of the way our brains are wired. It's just in our nature that we are the way we are. We are the nurturers that take care of the family, so it's in our character to cater to men. In the act of catering to him, there can be a misconception. He may start to think you're just doing it out of Love. The reality is that women cater to men because it makes us who we are. It gives us purpose to cook, clean, and take care of the family.

My Guide to Love & Romance

Life becomes more painful when you have to see the person because you have a child together. You have to be really strong in these cases, because there is a child involved. The worse thing we can do as adults is to openly show our petty quarrels in front of the children. It really confuses them, and creates mental problems for them as adults. They can develop serious social disorders that can become severe.

There will always be some form of resentment because one party got hurt more than the other. But in the end, both parties, men and women, feel the same human emotions.

Let me tell you something, a lot of men be frontin'. They feel the same pain women feel. You can act all tough and macho, but Mama Jones knows. Not to put my son on blast, but I've seen him distraught many times because he messed up and got caught cheating. Now he's coming to Mama because he feels terrible that he hurt the woman he loved. So we both feel pain. The difference between men and women is how we express our emotions.

Now that we have established when the timing isn't right for Love, now let's discuss when the timing is right for Love. You know when the timing is right, everything is perfect. You've been out of your relationship for at least six months, and you've given yourself time to recuperate from the old relationship. Let me say this, recovering from a bad relationship is similar to someone recuperating from a bad car accident. You can't just get up and walk away from an 80 miles-per-hour head-on collision. Well, it's the same with a relationship. The damage that has been done is mental, so it's deeper than any physical pain you can imagine. Mental anguish is the worst because you can't put a band aid on a mental wound. Sometimes a mental injury will take years to recover from, while a physical injury can be healed in six months to a year.

After you've healed from your last relationship, then think about getting back out into social life. You're finally feeling good about being single and you're ready to mingle. For the ladies, you're putting your favorite 'Freakum Dress' on, making sure everything is tight, right, and out of sight! For the fellows, you're making sure your hair cut is perfect, and your outfit is fly. And then the two of you meet at the club, sparks start to fly immediately. The conversation is stimulating, it's almost like there is no one in the club but the two of you. At the end of the night you exchange numbers and part ways.

The next day you can't wait to call to see if you'll both have the same feeling you had last night. The call goes well,

My Guide to Love & Romance

and you establish a date, and just like the night before, you hit it off. The timing was right. Nothing happens by coincidence or chance when it comes to Love. It was meant for you to be in the same place at the same time; the stars were aligned. As they say, the rest is history.

Until your healing period has ended, clear your thoughts. Don't think about a relationship or anything associated with one. Let time heal your heart and you'll be surprised. Love will find you. The timing has to be right, or there will be a glimpse of Love, but it won't be the real Love you seek. Like I said before, timing is everything, and when the time is right you'll find your true Love.

Here are some key points from this chapter to remember:

1. Timing is of the essence when it comes to finding Love & Romance.
2. The season has to be right. Nothing grows out of season—not even Love.
3. Give yourself time to heal after a bad break.
4. Be patient, know when the time is right to Love again.
5. Clear your mind before falling head over heels. Be sure that it's right to avoid the same thing.

My Guide to Love & Romance

It's important to follow the steps and tips in this book. Life is easier when we have help. You'll be surprised how a little wisdom will transform your life for the better.

CHAPTER 14

"Be Patient; Do it Right!
Patience is a virtue, so take your time."

Everyone is always in a rush to find Love & Romance. When you finally find it, most times you don't know what to do with it. Patience is the key. You must learn to take your time and do it right. Really take the time to do things with balance and focus, because Lord knows most of us don't even think on that level when we're in Love. Being in Love often places blinders on our vision, so we tend not to be conscious of certain things while in that space. When we make the conscious decision to take our time, for once in our lives, we see the benefits of it.

It took me years to figure out this simple concept. I was almost in my 40's when I realized that you can't rush Love. We all want to speed through Love's obstacle course. There is no finish line, but we pretend there is. The way to make Love

My Guide to Love & Romance

& Romance endure the test of time is very simple. TAKE YOUR TIME. Move with caution and savor every moment while you're in that space.

When I was younger, I would meet a man that I was attracted to and instantly fall in Love with him. Every time I did that, the relationship would never last. We both felt the same way, but we were too fast and the Love exhausted itself. You do know that Love can exhaust itself? That's right, Love exhausts itself when you move too fast. It's like running a marathon; only difference in this race is that the person that finishes first is in last place. In the race of Love, the object is not to finish the race fast; it is to take your time and move slow so it will last. When you get to the end, that's when you lose interest because you've just sped through it and the race is over. When it's over, it's over; there is no reset or another chance to sprint through the course. Most of us aren't conscious of how fast we're moving in a relationship. We just measure everything with self-gratification without realizing we're speeding.

There is no right way to be in Love, there is only the experience. We all learn from the actual experience of being in Love, so there is no other way to learn. I can only tell you what I understand about Love from my knowledge, but there

My Guide to Love & Romance

is no concrete way to teach. There is only the experience. I can teach you something from all my encounters, but every case is different. However, if you take notes and apply what I'm teaching in this guide, I can guarantee that you'll have at least an 80% chance at success. The other 20% is unforeseen circumstances that can get in the way of us understanding how to move in Love land.

So, when you finally find Love, you want to do it right so it will last. We have established that there is no right way to be in Love, but there is a right way to take your time, which in essence, is doing it the right way. There are a few steps that I want to point out in reference to taking your time and doing it the right way.

STEP 1. MOVE WITH CAUTION. When you move with caution you're moving at a very measured pace. Calculate every move so that it's in accordance with your objective, which is creating that space for Love & Romance.

STEP 2. PRACTICE PATIENCE. Treat your new prospect as though you are the most patient person on Earth. You will develop the patience that you project by practicing fortitude.

My Guide to Love & Romance

There is nothing more anti-seductive than a person who is rushing someone to fall in Love with them. Just because you're ready to jump off a cliff doesn't mean I am.

STEP 3. SAVOR THE MOMENTS.

Understand that each moment you're in Love is precious within itself. Like I mentioned before, there is a special measure of time for Lovers. Time moves fast when you're having fun, especially when you're in Love. It will seem like the time is literally speeding because the experience of Love is so enjoyable and exciting. Relish every special moment that you're in Love.

I'm serious when I say that in Love land time is very different. I remember being in deep Love with Mundy, and I'll tell you, I don't know where the time went. All those special moments we shared feel like it was yesterday, but it happened so fast that my head spins just thinking about it. We met, fell in Love, had two children, fell out of Love, then fell back in Love and then he died in the span of twenty-five years. All that in one sentence, and that's how fast time in Love land moves.

Close your eyes for a minute and think about your most fond memories of time shared with someone you Love. You

My Guide to Love & Romance

can feel something deep when you do that; it's therapeutic in a way. Just to be able to go there at will is amazing to say the least. That goes to show you how valuable time is when it's shared in Love. The memories make you smile and take you to that space instantly.

We all deserve to have romantic times with our mates. It's what makes being in a relationship worth it. I remember all the romantic times I shared with Mundy, just snuggled up in his arms lying on his chest. Or just taking a walk through the park and sitting on the bench talking for hours. I miss those times, but I can always visit them in my mind. That is the difference between lust and Romance, lust is so forgettable, when romance is forever memorable.

So, what did we learn today? You should be soaking up some good lessons by now on this journey. I really hope you're paying attention because Love is a serious matter. It is the difference between being happy, or living a life of misery. Pick your poison. For me, I've already chosen to live my life on the happy side of things, because I don't have time to be a pessimist or a hater. It's never been my thing to be negative. I'm no angel, but I'm pretty damn close to it. I'm just joking.

My Guide to Love & Romance

Lord knows that I'm no angel, but he also knows that my heart is good, so that's the balance.

I've learned a lot of things about life, but one of the simplest lessons that seems to be the most complex is how to Love. I would be lying to you if I told you that I had the absolute fool proof blueprint to Love & Romance. Unlike some other so-called Love experts with relationship books out (I'm not saying any names); I'm sincere when I say no one can guarantee you a life of Love and Happiness. I'm going to keep it all the way real with you if I don't do anything else.

I believe in God, and God is Love to me. It is because of God that I'm able to relate His messages to you. These are more than just some words about Love & Romance; they're really words of divine inspiration sent from God himself. I've been through so much in my life, and I know God has had his hands on me, guiding me through the rough times. This book is a testament to that fact, because truth be told I'm not supposed to be here speaking like this. In my autobiography I will tell my story, but for now I'm just doing what God wants me to do, which is teach the masses how to Love again.

This will conclude this section on Be Patient; Do it Right. I've learned a lot just writing this part of the book. It's amazing when you make connections to things that you've

My Guide to Love & Romance

never contemplated before. Again, use your time wisely, ladies and gentlemen, while you're not in a relationship. Occupy your time by doing things that are positive, like charity walks for cancer, or helping with blood drives, or feeding the homeless. Doing something that is selfless will nourish your soul. Well, it's time to move on to the next section of this amazing voyage. Are you enjoying it so far? I sincerely hope so.

Ladies, this next section is strictly for you. And girl do I have a lot on my mind for you. I'm going to let you have it as if you were my daughter because I Love you. So now get ready for a little tough Love.

PART IV

STRICTLY FOR THE LADIES!

CHAPTER 15

"Respect Yourself!
If you don't respect yourself, no one will."

W hen I decided to call this part of the book STRICTLY FOR THE LADIES, I had to take a deep breath. My mind said, "Where should I begin?" And that's when the word respect just popped into my head. Respect is a big word. In fact it's more than just a word it's a concept. Respect implies that you have dignity, that you are considerate of others as well as your place in this world. However, in this chapter I'm cutting straight to the point. Women, you have to respect yourself better than you have been. I'm not judging anyone. I'm just calling a spade a spade.

I see how it's going down nowadays with the young women. It is atrocious! The things women are doing today make all women look shameful. The self-disrespect is hideous, to the point that men today can do pretty much what they want. All you have to do is watch a group of young women and listen to the way they talk and act.

I do take into account that things are very different now as opposed to back in my day. Social media is a gift and a curse. The gift is being able to trade information rapidly. The curse is the immoral things it allows people to do. Some women are openly showing naked pictures of themselves to the world on Facebook. All a guy has to do now is browse Facebook and find the freaky girls by the pictures they post. Leave a little message in the in-box, and just like that, she is coming to see you for sex.

Ladies, please stop fucking putting naked pictures up on the Internet for everyone to see. Don't you think that makes you look cheap and easy when you do that? It's bad when releasing sex-tapes on the Internet makes you a celebrity. This sends the wrong message to the millions of young women out there. Now you see all these young ladies out here thinking that putting half-naked pictures on the Internet is a way to get attention. You're getting the wrong attention, so STOP! You're making all of us look bad.

It seems like social media has made the divide between men and women even wider. You would think the invention of

My Guide to Love & Romance

social media would bring man and woman closer, but it's quite the opposite. Social media is hypersexual, so it has increased all sexuality. There is so much sex on the net that you can hook up with any type of woman you desire.

Pussy used to have great value. Now it's reduced to nothing because of all the promiscuous women of the world that are giving it away for free. When I say pussy had great value, I don't mean that in terms of selling it. I've never been for that. I mean the great value that men placed on it. There was a time that a man would beg a woman for some pussy, and damn near bend over backward to get some. When I say some, I mean just a little bit. He had to do a couple more back flips and somersaults before he could get a little bit more. We made a man value the time of day we spent with them; they had to show enormous respect. That's one of the things that is missing all around the board, RESPECT.

And I hate to say it, but ladies, it's our fault that these men are acting the way they do. You see, back in the day we had a general consensus as women. It was not tolerating disrespect. We demanded respect and showed it in return. It's a two way street, so the more respectful men were, the women were equally respectful. Men were big on chivalry back then, which made it easier to get along with them. Today, some men

My Guide to Love & Romance

couldn't care less about chivalry. What happened to the men? I'll get into that in the next part of this book, but for now let's stick to the ladies.

These days it seems like a contest between men and women to see who can be the most disrespectful, low-down person. It has turned into a cesspool where anything goes. It is really disappointing because there are so many beautiful young women out there that I see when I travel. They are all like my daughters. My heart pours out to them when I see them, because I know what type of world this is today. That is why I'm here; I know I will reach some of the young women and change the way they perceive Love & Romance.

Respect starts with self. The first lesson of respect is that if you don't respect yourself, no man is ever going to respect you. No matter what, you can have a master's degree from Yale, all the money and success, but if you let a man disrespect you and you tolerate it, you're a dummy. We've all been there, but I have to call it what it is. We were all being stupid. Being in a state of denial about the truth only prolongs the cycle. If he disrespects you and you allow it, he's going to continue.

Mama Jones
My Guide to Love & Romance

The interesting thing about this vicious sequence of events is the mental ramifications it has on a woman's self-image. When anyone disrespects you it's painful, but when it's a man you Love, it's ten times more detrimental. Women become victims of vicious emotional assaults when they allow men to disrespect them. It has gotten worse for women in the last ten to twenty years. The woman's liberation movement has suffered blow after staggering blow. We have taken so many steps backward that we may as well be doing the moonwalk, because there is nothing positive going on. There are more half-naked women shaking their ass than at any time in history. This is devastating. What does the future hold for women? At the rate that we're moving backward, I wouldn't be surprised if they reinstate the wife-beating law. Did you know it was legal to beat your wife in this country? There used to be a law in America that stated that a man could beat his wife with a stick no longer than the length of his hand. If he beat her with a stick that was bigger than the length of his hand there was a fine. Can you believe it? We've come a long way since the days that we couldn't vote, when we were considered second class citizens. Things can go back to those days if we don't enlighten these young women of the world today.

Mama Jones
My Guide to Love & Romance

News flash, ladies. It is a reflection of how you see yourself when you let a man treat you in any fashion. Sometimes it's deep issues with an absent father, or other life-changing experiences, but the women who allow this have a mental disorder. I know that sounds extreme, but it's the truth. Some women think they deserve to be treated in a disrespectful way because that's all they know. They mistake disrespect as Love, when it's the total opposite of Love. A man that disrespects his woman thinks this behavior is acceptable because his woman doesn't correct it.

Ladies, every one of you are first and foremost Queens in your own right. A Queen must respect herself at all times. The minute she forgets this, she is denying her own existence, and has immediately fallen from grace. Always remember this, because the next time a man disrespects you, tell him that if he ever does it again his head will be chopped off for disrespecting a Queen. Say it like you mean it, not like some peasant. And if he doesn't take you serious, symbolically chop his head off by cutting him off. No more phone calls, no sex, no interaction at all. The next time he's about to disrespect a woman, he'll think twice about it.

My Guide to Love & Romance

These are the things young ladies need to be discussing; not who has a big dick and what kind of car such and such has. You are all selling yourselves short. You could be getting the utmost respect if you all knew how to stick together and show the men that you're not having that shit anymore! Trust me, the men will have no choice but to straighten up and fly right if they ever want to be intimate with a woman again. I know the idea is farfetched because trying to get women to stick together is like getting cats to hang with dogs. Women are so catty with each other. That's why it's hard for us to restore femininę order.

Never fear, Mama Jones is here to save the day, all is not lost. We can bring it back to the glory days of old. Sisters, we must unite as one! Are you with me! If you're reading this book then that is a step in the right direction for all women.

I'm not about male bashing; however, I am about women's empowerment. Women are not second class citizens; we're mothers, sisters, aunts. We nurture children and maintain households; a man should never disrespect you. Every man came from a woman, so what gives him the right to think he can treat us with anything other than nobility.

Mama Jones
My Guide to Love & Romance

So ladies, if you're reading this book, can we agree on a few things? This will be sort of like a pact between you and Mama Jones. Repeat after me:

1. We will respect ourselves at all times from this day forward.
2. We will stick together on matters that concern women as a whole.
3. When a man disrespects us, we will warn him one time. The next time he does it, off with his head.
4. We will stop hating and being so catty with one another.
5. We will always carry ourselves like the Queens we are.
6. Stop throwing each other under the bus!

Now ladies, after you've made this pact with Mama Jones, you're obligated to carry out your oath. The penalty is death to anyone that breaks any one of the tenants set forth in my pact. Is that clear?

Just joking, you won't die if you break any of the points in our pact. I just want you all to take Mama Jones serious. I think you'll be okay once you've gotten this far in my guide. There is still more to go, so stay with me.

My Guide to Love & Romance

In a world where men basically oppress women, we need to stick together. We're stronger as a unit than we are divided. We can change the world for the better if we stand strong for issues that concern us all. As we speak, the Texas state government is trying to take away a woman's right to have an abortion. This is a woman's choice, not the choice of some group of men that know nothing about child birth. If we were unified, there would be no debate.

CHAPTER 16

"Control Your Emotions!
Crazy with emotions? Practice self-control."

L et me tell you something. Men are really simple creatures; we are the ones that complicate things with our emotions. We can get crazy with our emotions, ladies. I know from experience. I learned to control my emotions over the years. It takes a lot of practice, but you can do it too. It's a very difficult thing to do because we are emotional creatures by nature. So it's kind of like asking you to be something other than yourself, but it's essential that you control your emotions for the survival of Love with a man.

Men aren't as emotional as women, so they automatically view emotions as a weakness. In essence, becoming emotional is a weakness because it clouds judgment. When we get all emotional we make hasty decisions that we wouldn't have made in our right state of mind. It confuses men when they can't understand us. Hell, I would be confused too if I were a man. One minute I'm hot, the next I'm cold. Sometimes we can be so emotional that it creates anti-seductive behavior without us even knowing it. It's true, ladies, we have to start admitting when things are not so balanced.

Nevertheless, these are small things that can be worked on. When I was a younger woman I was an emotional wreck at times. I was young, so I didn't understand what I was feeling. My body was changing, so my hormones were out of control. I always had my mother around me to teach me how to be a lady, so that's where I got the balance. She taught me how to control my emotions when I'm angry. I was taught to be on my best behavior at all times when I was very young, and I taught my daughters. Throughout the years I learned that controlling your emotions help you to keep a clear mind as well. It's almost like a tradition, because I know my daughters are going to pass down the lessons.

Young ladies of the world, if you don't have a real woman around to mentor you on becoming a lady, then you're probably not a lady at all. Once again, that's the reason Mama Jones is here. I'm personally giving every young woman reading this book my permission to use me as your personal mentor. I will use all my wisdom to guide you in the right direction. Now, I don't want anyone reading this to take it the wrong way. Do not show up at my house talking about, "You said I have permission to use you as my personal mentor." I'm liable to lose it at times, but all jokes aside, you're all Mama's babies, and I want all of you to find true Love and Happiness.

When I say it takes everything that I am to keep from going completely bonkers sometimes, that is an understatement. I have to take deep breaths and take a walk and I still want to blow up. Recently, I've been losing my cool, and I couldn't figure out what was wrong with me. I went to the doctor to get checked out; you never know when something is internally wrong.

I lost two family members to cancer, my sister and my mother. They didn't know until the last minute when it was too late. Breast cancer is no joke. It kills hundreds of women every year. I am an avid cancer awareness advocate. I visit cancer patients and do charity walks and other cancer awareness events. If my mother and my sister would've went to get checked out sooner, they would be here today. Ladies, it's very important that you get screened for cancer regularly. It is literally the difference between life and death.

My Guide to Love & Romance

So when the doctor finished my examination, he told me that I was healthy but there was one thing he had to tell me. "Have a seat, Mrs. Jones." The way he spoke made me nervous. "I have something to tell you." He paused, which made me more nervous. "You're going through menopause."

I was like, "Wow!" I didn't think it was something like that, but I am fifty-four years old, so it's bound to happen sooner or later. The menopause was toying with my emotions, so much that I would yell and scream one minute and then cry the next. Oh, my God, I've never been this emotional in my life. I'm learning to cope with it, but it is a lesson of life that I want to share with you as a teaching tool. I'm not ashamed of my age, or the fact that I'm going through menopause.

On the contrary, I'm happy to be alive at my age, because like I said before, Lord knows I'm not supposed to be here. I've been on the streets doing drugs, running with dangerous men that ended up getting killed because of the lifestyle. I've sold drugs to feed my family. I'm not proud of any of this. I'm merely explaining to you a little about my past.

However, the lesson I've learned that I want to share with you ladies is how to control your emotions without contradicting your nature. In fact, you'll be adding luster to your character. When we learn the art of patience, fortitude,

My Guide to Love & Romance

and tolerance, we transcend the need to act on emotions. These are just three powerful virtues that can help you, not only with your emotions, but they will transform you into the beautiful butterfly God intended you to be.

I get chills just thinking about how powerful the mind is, and how one idea can alter your whole existence. Just by thinking about controlling your emotions, you are programming your mind to perform the function; it is a gift from the Father. We need to start recognizing that the things we think of on a daily basis plays a part in what will happen in our lives. Positive thoughts create positive actions, which in turn creates the space that we call happiness. In that space there is Love, Romance, health, wealth and all the things your heart desires. It's all about finding that space or creating it. Some people have a garden or a sea shore that they can physically go to, and that becomes the "space" I speak on. Whatever works for you, as long as you find it. Then once you've found it, learn how to stay there, or go there at will.

There are not many people that can really grasp this whole concept. So if you're a person reading this and you catch on easily, consider yourself one of the few. Just the fact that you're even reading this book tells me that you can grasp these concepts. I was told a long time ago, "Readers are Leaders!" So welcome to the club, because I Love to read.

Ladies, by controlling your emotions you become graceful, and your quality of life increases for the better. When you're emotional all the time, your quality of life is very poor because you've created a negative space. I'm always speaking about creating that positive space for yourself, but you do know that you can inadvertently construct a very negative space. You can be in that space without knowing it; before you know it, years have passed. Being too emotional can make you miserable as well.

Here are a few suggestions:

1. Clear your mind; let your conscious be free.
2. Use your positive mantra to create the positive space.
3. Meditate daily.
4. Stay focused on maintaining and staying in that space.

While you're on your journey you will be tested. People will see you attempting to be positive, and they will try to throw a monkey wrench in the machine. Be aware of the test, if not, you'll fail every time. As long as you're conscious of the haters you will be able to sidetrack them instead of them sidetracking you. The main focus is to remain on the path. When you've reached the finish line, rejoice in your patience to reach the goals you've set for yourself.

So we always want to be in the best place possible. No one wants to be miserable or negative, but sometimes you're not conscious of what's actually going on in your life. With a degree of control you also become aware of the subtle things that are happening in your life. You know most of us women are really not aware of our emotions and how it plays a part of who we are. When you realize these things, pay attention to them so you can have a measure of control over your emotions. Like I said, controlling my emotions was one of the hardest things I had to do as a woman. However, I understand the importance of it, so I've made it my business to practice controlling my emotions and being more conscious of how I move. Trust me. You'll witness your life change in the blink of an eye.

Now, I want to touch base on some things that I spoke on in this chapter. These are some of the virtues I'd like for you to practice. By simply repeating these powerful virtues in your mind, you're programming yourself to act on them. It's a very easy process with maximum benefits. It is a great exercise to

My Guide to Love & Romance

contemplate on the virtues of life. You'll find yourself becoming more positive and light on your feet as you progress.

Just by reading the virtues that I've set forth, you're also imbedding them into your mind. If you go over them once a day for two weeks, you will have programmed your subconscious to initiate a sequence of thought patterns. These thought patterns will be on a subconscious level, so you won't be aware of them working on your mind. You'll just see the results as they manifest themselves in your life.

List of Virtues:

Fortitude - When we practice fortitude we become resilient in our endeavors. We develop the stamina to endure, and the courage to face life's truths head on.

Tolerance - With tolerance we develop an open mind; an open mind is more susceptible to grasping life's lessons.

Patience - With patience we learn to persevere through the storms of life. Sometimes patience gives Love staying power as opposed to running a race where Love burns itself out.

Steadfastness – Gives you the devotion to be dedicated in a loving relationship. By exercising steadfastness you are being resolute and determined to stay loyal.

My Guide to Love & Romance

Study these virtues and internalize them. Watch as they work on your mindset. You will feel a sense of wisdom that will help you become the wise woman you set out to be. It is all about you and your relationship with God at the end of the day. It is the first Love affair every woman should have, a Love affair with God Almighty. Only He can show you the way.

Also, God is a God of reason. Just as He has some pastors feeding his flock, He has also blessed some individuals with a great college education and the experience to assist sisters and brothers facing serious emotional and mental issues. So if you are experiencing depression or some other mental or emotional issues that seem too weighty where you feel as if you are losing control or don't have a grasp on reality, then don't be afraid to seek out a professional for mental health services.

Below is a list of mental health resources and support groups:

1. Mental Health America,
   www.mentalhealthamerica.net

2. NAMI: National Alliance on Mental Illness, Mental Health Support Groups,
   www.nami.org
3. Psych Central: Mental Health Support Groups,
   www.psychcentral.com
4. Anxiety and Depression Association of America,
   www.adaa.org

CHAPTER 17

"Keep Your Head Up!
The miracle of life starts with women, always demand
a level of respect."

L adies, I know it's hard out here being a woman in today's world. Disrespect for women is at an all-time high. Never before have I witnessed the mass degradation of the female species. I spoke about this earlier, but I must reiterate my views because they are so important. As women we have dropped the ball when it comes to the respect we deserve. So at the end of the day there is no one to blame but us. We let men carry on as if we don't deserve to be respected.

When a man cheats on you and you give him another chance, that's understandable. Even a murderer can be forgiven once, but when your man is a persistent cheater, he deserves the death penalty, which means to cut him off completely. When you allow him to stay, you're co-signing his behavior. Once he knows he can misbehave and get away with it, all you're going to do is cry and ask why. Because you let him, that's why!

The disrespect for women is evident, especially in Hip Hop. It's so demeaning to hear some of the lyrics rappers spew about women. Rappers have helped destroy the image of the woman by constantly showing us as sexual objects that have no value. If you rely on rap songs and the rap videos to shape your opinion of women, you would say that all women are nothing but bitches and hoes that should be subject to being belittled and humiliated for a man's enjoyment.

My own son is a culprit of this act, and I've told him about it time and time again. He has slowed down with it, but he's still on his male chauvinist tip. I didn't teach Jelmoe to be that way. I taught him to treat women with respect and dignity. It is this rap shit that has made my son the way he is. I taught him better than that, but anyway, he's still my only son, so I don't judge him.

But this message is strictly for the ladies; I'll get to the fellows in Part V. Ladies, do me a favor. Stop letting these men get away with this bullshit they've been doing. Enough is enough! The only reason men continue to act in this manner is

My Guide to Love & Romance

because we keep allowing it. And ladies stop buying into this nonsense about there being a shortage of Black men. That's why most of you put up with the crap, because you actually believe there isn't enough Black men to go around. Ask the White woman if there's a shortage of Black men.

We could put a stop to the shit once and for all. We have to stop being catty with one another and stick together on the important issues that affect women as a whole. We need to be stern in our relationships with men. We have to start standing up for women's rights. Together we can make a change.

For instance, if you meet a man and he says he's married or in a relationship, but he still wants to hang out with you on the side, tell him no. We have to start taking into consideration that his woman is your kindred sister, and messing with this man is wrong. You don't have to know the woman; all you have to know is that she is just like you. She is going to be devastated just like you'd be if you were in Love and your man betrayed you. And to avoid the inevitable humiliation when he's tired of playing with you and he tosses you to the side like a ragdoll.

What I want you to do in spite of all the turmoil going on in the world is 'Keep Your Head Up.' I have always loved that message that the late great Tupac Shakur sung about so brilliantly. That song is what made me start paying attention to him. That's what I want you to do for me, hold your head high.

Although you may be fatherless, or maybe your biological father isn't in your life, you all have a spiritual Father that you can call on. You are all daughters of the Most High God, and he wants us all to be happy and in Love. I know what you're all going through, and believe me, it's not easy being a woman. This is what God made you, so rejoice in the grace of your divine femininity. It is a blessing to be able to give birth; it's a blessing to have that motherly instinct. We are Queens, and Goddesses of the Universe! That is more than enough reason to celebrate womanhood. A man should NEVER DISRESPECT A WOMAN! SHE IS YOUR MOTHER, YOUR WIFE, YOUR AUNT, AND YOUR SISTER!

So when you're feeling down because of the way things seem to be in the world, remember these wise words from Mama Jones. "You are beautiful, so let your beauty radiate from the inside out, and to the whole world."

There are times when I just can't take it anymore. I mean, I want to just go crazy sometimes when I see how women are treated. Especially the young women of today; they have it the

My Guide to Love & Romance

worse. Like I mentioned before, men used to have the utmost admiration for women. I don't know what happened to these new age men. They simply have no regard for the female species whatsoever. It could be the social media, or just the times. Whatever it is, this has to stop. We need to have open conversations about how to Love each other.

I have four daughters. I pray for them every night that God will keep them in His everlasting arms and protect them in this cruel world that is almost anti-female. I might be going to the extreme with that last statement, however, it seems that way at times. I mean, things have somewhat gotten better. But it's not the men alone who are perpetuating the disrespect of women. Women are promoting their own demise.

Women, keep your head up. This is a demand from Mama Jones! Across the globe I want all the women to hear me! Hold your head up high, respect yourself, and show the world that we are the Queens we are meant to be. This is the best time to be alive. We are about to witness something very special in this lifetime. I can't put my finger on it, but it's something that I just feel.

If there is a woman out there reading this book that may be going through some deep issues, I hope this book reaches you and touches you in that deep space. We need to be mindful of each other's struggle. We can change the condition of the world. This current world is spiraling into oblivion, especially with the way morality keeps rapidly decreasing. I've witnessed a lot in my life, and one thing is for sure, the world is not right nowadays. I feel it in the air. Maybe it is the end of the world, because there is a chill I get that makes me tremble sometimes. I'm not trying to divert from the topic by being prophetic; I just felt like throwing that out there because it corresponds with my message.

I see the babies and I wonder what kind of world will they live in when they grow up. I won't be here, but my grandchildren will. I want them to live in a world that's worth living in. I don't like the way things are looking. I do believe that we can do something about it. We don't have to just sit and watch the world fall into decay. I'll be damned if I just sit idle.

That's what this book is really about, my attempt to change the whole world for the better. I can't explain this deep inner feeling I have for making the world a beautiful place filled with Love for everyone. After all, we are all ONE, whether you agree or not. It's not up for debate! I don't care if you're a White, Latin, Chinese, Black, etc., WE ALL COME FROM

Mama Jones
My Guide to Love & Romance

THE SAME SOURCE, WHICH IS GOD! There is no one group better than the next. We are all children of God! Men and women alike, all we need to understand is that when I disrespect you I'm disrespecting myself. We have to get back to the basics, the foundation, which is that good old fashioned Love. It's not hard to do, it's easier than it seems. It's actually harder to hate because it goes against our true nature which is to Love.

Here are some steps you can take toward healing:

1. Visit onyxwoman.com to join the Fatherless daughters group for information on counseling.
2. Confront your father and ask for a reunion.
3. Don't feel terrible if your father doesn't respond positively.
4. Keep in mind that you don't need anyone to make you happy. Having a relationship with your biological father is a natural act of completion.

I have one statement that will be the most important six words in this chapter.

Together we can change the world.

CHAPTER 18

"The Lady Code!
The Rules and Regulations of being a real lady."

Too many women out here go directly against the 'Lady Code'. The Lady Code is my terminology for the rules and regulations of being a real lady. Most of our mothers taught us the basics of being a lady, but it seems that knowledge has faded, so I'm going to bring it back to the forefront. It's time for a refresher course, ladies. I know some of you think you know everything, especially you young ladies. I raised four girls, so I know how you girls get when you start smelling yourself.

Sometimes all a girl needs is to be informed about the subject and they catch on immediately. But what if there is no one out there informing the masses of young women about the ways of a lady? You will end up with a situation like the one the world is in at the present moment, chaos. That's the problem, not enough older women are out there beating the

171

My Guide to Love & Romance

trail and showing these young girls the virtuous ways of womanhood. That's why God appointed me to do the job of enlightening the youth with this guide.

If you let TV teach these girls anything, they're going to be nothing but whores! And that's the problem. We're letting the idiot box teach our young girls how to become the wrong kind of woman. They are watching *The Bad Girls Club*, and all these other shows that display behavior that is unbecoming of a lady, and it is very misleading. Now you see why they're acting the way they do. They're imitating what they see on TV.

These young girls are out here fighting each other like animals. All you have to do is go on *WorldStar Hip Hop* and see all these young girls beating the hell out of each other. It's really sad because if they only knew their worth. Well, I'm not going to bash them too much because it's not all their fault. We have to take some of the blame as adults. Something went wrong somewhere.

I believe that if enough young women are able to change their ways, we can uplift the whole world. All we have to do is restore the Lady Code. I know that sounds a bit exaggerated, but it's not. Back in the day the woman regulated everything in the relationship. Most of you can't go back that far, but

My Guide to Love & Romance

there was a time when women did the choosing, and it was up to the woman whether there was going to be anything popping off. I mentioned before how men had to beg and bend over backward just to get a kiss, let alone sex. When a man finally got sex, he was so appreciative that he continued to treat his woman like royalty because he wanted more sex.

What that did was make the man conscious of his lady, and he treated her with the utmost respect. Women were held in the highest regards, and any decent man knew he had to come correct if he wanted the companionship of a lady. Now, he could go get him a two dollar whore on any street corner, but if he wanted a lady, he had to bring his A-game, baby.

I don't know what happened, or where the tables turned, but things are totally different nowadays. Men don't feel the need to treat women with the utmost respect. They talk to women as if they're entitled to treat us any way they want because women have forgotten, or don't know about the Lady Code.

Yes, women of the world today are more assertive as opposed to back in the day. They're more independent and feel they don't need a man in their lives. I think that attitude is one of the things that has destroyed the respect of the Lady

Code. When a woman feels she doesn't need a man in her life, then she loses her ladyship. And the Lady Code began to decline into what we see today. Some of these women are not ladies, but despicable tramps and sluts that will fuck anything with a penis. They have no morals and no code of ethics. Anything goes with the women of today. And the men know it, that's why they don't put in any work when it comes to getting a woman.

These new women violate the entire Lady Code. Like I said, they have no code. They don't care about being respected by men or women for that matter. These renegade 'hos of today don't give a damn how anyone sees them; they are just lost. You'll hear a lot of women saying that women are worse than men these days. That's because they lack the knowledge of a real woman. When a woman knows her self-worth, she naturally follows the Lady Code.

Now, allow me to put into writing my infamous **Lady Code.** It's common sense, but like I said before: Sense isn't that common anymore. Just like everything else in this book, the Lady Code isn't written in stone. What it is, is a blueprint for women to build their confidence and to bring back the ways of a Lady. Before I die, I will make a difference and it starts now!

My Guide to Love & Romance

The Lady Code

1. Always carry yourself with respect.
2. Never date a married man, or a man that is in any type of relationship.
3. Never date any of your friends' ex-boyfriends.
4. If your girl is talking to a man, don't get intimate with him.
5. Never blow your cool, stay calm and collected under any situation.
6. When you meet a man, make him wait at least six months for sex.
7. Present yourself with royalty, and he will follow suit.
8. Stay away from renegade 'hos; they will taint your image.
9. Have compassion for humanity.
10. Enjoy life, smile and be happy, and let your lady-like aura radiate unto the world.

Love is always the answer in any situation, so I'm going to keep it on track. A true lady must first Love herself, because it's the foundation to real growth and development. When we

Mama Jones
My Guide to Love & Romance

Love ourselves life becomes easier. Things in life can be very challenging, but with a little guidance we can balance it out. That's what I'm all about, balance. Without balance, life is out of course.

With the right direction we can restore our honor as ladies. It saddens me to see all these young women out here lost, and being severely disrespected. I understand why we do what we do: we want to be loved by men, so we settle for the treatment just to be in a relationship. No one wants to be lonely, but being in a non-loving relationship is worse than being lonely. Hell, I'd rather be lonely than let anyone treat me any old way, not Mama Jones!

Love yourself, ladies! Everything will fall into place once we Love who we are wholeheartedly. We have to figure out the dynamics of ourselves first before we get intimate with a man. Men are very simple, yet very complex. When we figure out these important lessons is when we become what God intended.

Well, ladies, it's been real speaking with you. This will conclude Part IV. I hope that I was helpful in addressing the ladies in this part. I am sincere when I say that I Love each and every one of you with all my heart. Ladies, please take heed to my wisdom; embrace it as a gospel because it is.

Mama Jones
My Guide to Love & Romance

These words are not just some sentences and phrases just to fill up space in my book. Every word I utter is important, and my intentions are the most righteous.

When this guide is done and in print, I will rejoice and praise God. I know this is His workings, and I don't want the glory for something God is doing. You will understand when it is all said and done, because at the end of the day it's all about restoring the balance. Lord knows the world needs to be healed and repaired.

One last thing before I go. Ladies, stop referring to yourselves as Bitches, 'Hos, and Hookers. If you dislike it when men refer to you as those names, then don't turn around and refer to yourself or your friend by those same names. I even heard my youngest daughter call her friend "slut" as a term of endearment. It's disgusting! If you want to be treated like a Queen, then find a better way to identify with one another.

Well, that is all for the ladies. Now it's time to get at the fellows. Oh, boy, do I have my hands full with you guys. You're a mess, but Mama is going to clean it up. We're going to get it together one way or another!

PART V

STRICTLY

FOR THE

FELLOWS!

CHAPTER 19

Be A Real Man!
"I'm a grown ass man, so what I still live with my
Mama." Try again.

ellows, I'm cutting straight to the chase with you guys. I raised a boy into a man. I did the best I could to cultivate Jelmoe into a real man. Sometimes I think I could've done a better job, but for the most part I think I did okay. I tried to show him how to be a real man, but what I was really doing was showing him my idea of what a real man is, because I'm not a man. Only a man can show another male how to be a man, but a woman is qualified to teach a boy how to be a respectful human being.

But I'm talking to you, yeah you. The so-called man that lies to women, makes babies and deserts them, leaving them for dead. The so-called man, the coward that beats his woman and doesn't work; he just freeloads off women. The so-called man that still lives with his mother, but every chance he gets he's screaming, "I'm a grown ass man!" Do Mama Jones a big favor. Shut the fuck up! BE A REAL MAN!

How to Be a Real Man

You are a disgrace to the male species—the nerve of you to really consider yourself a real man. You're obviously delusional, because you're not the real deal by far. You parade around pretending to be something you're not, because a real man is noble and he has integrity. And by the way, a real man doesn't have to run around saying, "I'm a grown ass man!" A real man doesn't have to validate or prove his manhood to anyone, so stating the evident is irrelevant.

It's been going on for too long; these men have been getting away with murder. No one is pulling their cards on the way they treat women. They are allowed to present themselves as men, even though they violate all the rules of being a real man. In fact, most of these deadbeats get justification from the rest of society. Because of the double standard, these so-called men are able to exist without being stoned or something. I really despise these types of men because they mess it up for the whole male species.

Mama Jones
My Guide to Love & Romance

Domestic Violence

This is a subject that is close to my heart because I've been in that situation where a man disrespected me. It's not a good feeling to be the victim of abuse, be it verbal, emotional, or physical. When a man that knows he is physically stronger than a woman, decides he wants to pummel her for whatever reason. It's dead wrong! It has to stop! A REAL MAN DOESN'T HIT WOMEN! ONLY COWARDS HIT WOMEN!

I know these men need help with this mental disorder. Most men that victimize women were victims themselves. Either they were abused by their fathers and watched him abuse the mother, or they didn't have a real man around to show them the ways of a real man. So some of this behavior is not their fault, however, that's no excuse to keep doing it. When is it going to really stop? We all have to step up and say something to these men. Enough is enough!

Fellows, I know that society says men can do what they want, but Mama Jones is here to say you can't do what you want anymore. I'm calling out all real men to join Mama Jones in a campaign to put a stop to the abusing of women by

My Guide to Love & Romance

so-called men. Real men, stand up and put a stop to this, because the so-called men of the world are corrupting the pure image of the real man. The real man is almost extinct!

I truly believe if real men ban together with real women that want to make a change, we can make a big difference in the world. By not saying anything at all, we're all enabling the actions of these males. Let's face it. Males have the power to change the world if they want to. We can't sit by idle while a group of so-called men continue to destroy the fabric of male/female relationships. You have to understand that these abusive males ruin good women and cause them to carry that experience over to the real man that wants a loving relationship.

Some women are so damaged that they can meet the best man on earth and they still won't be able to function normally in a relationship. The damage is so severe that the thought of being deceived again causes mental and physical pain. Can you imagine being tricked by men your whole life and then one man claims to be true? The chances of that woman believing him wholeheartedly are slimmer than pants on an anorexic model.

Mama Jones
My Guide to Love & Romance

This is a serious situation that must be addressed. I sincerely believe we have to put a stop to the abuse. I know it's hazardous getting involved in someone's relationship, but how long will we just let it happen? When you see or hear a woman getting her brains bashed in, real man, step up and do something. Nine times out of ten, a male who is beating on a woman is a pussy, so all a real man has to do is say something and he'll stop. We just can't let it go down anymore!

What is a real man? A real man is a man that is honest and forthcoming about his feelings. He doesn't lie just to get sex; he is beyond that. A real man treats a woman like a Queen, because he sees himself as a King and acts accordingly. When a real man gets his mate pregnant, he doesn't run from his responsibility. He does what he has to do to provide for the family. A real man is always respectful and commands the same respect that he gives. He stands firm on his principles and his passions are intense. I can keep going, but this is a summary of Mama Jones' definition of a real man.

Sometimes I find myself asking, "Where are all the real men?" I mean, it seems the world is overflowing with males masquerading as men. The fact that you have a penis qualifies you to be a male, but to be a man requires some of the characteristics that I spoke of. There used to be an abundance of real men in the world. No disrespect to the men of today, but times were just different back in my day. You had to man-up early in life, so I guess that made being a real man somewhat of a trend. If you were showing characteristics of the so-called man of today, then you were the outcast. Nowadays it's the total opposite; no one cares to call you out for not being a real man. Will the real men please stand up!

I do believe the males that have been violating the Man Code can be corrected with the right guidance from a real man. My sympathy does extend to some of these males; I don't think they're all bad. I know I started this chapter with a rant against certain types of males, but I had to get it off my chest. Actually, I think some of them can be saved, and that's what this is all about. I know it seems as though this chapter is all about bashing men that I feel aren't real. On the contrary, I want to help these individuals. If a killer can be forgiven, so can a so-called man.

The best way to help someone with these types of disorders is to first tell them about themselves. Then they have to admit that their behavior is wrong and has to be changed. Recognizing that there is a problem is essential to addressing the problem. It's just like a drug addict, they have to be honest and open about the issues. If you're a man, or you know a man that falls into this category, tell them there is help. Don't be ashamed. Get help because your behavior is unacceptable.

A man has to know that it's wrong to abuse a woman, or anyone for that matter. I feel like these types of men don't get a fair shake to fix the problem. We automatically throw them away without even trying to address the problem. Mama Jones is here to show compassion, but not without a little tough Love to go with it. I don't believe in doing anything nice and easy, that's not how I was raised. Having a tough life is what made me who I am today. Yes, my life is great now. I have money and fame, but shit wasn't always sweet. That's the reason I'm so raw.

Listen, when you are about to strike your woman, take a deep breath and walk away. I know you're probably accustomed to beating her, but if you really Love her then don't abuse her anymore. She loves you; that's why she stays with you and puts up with the vicious treatment. She prays that it'll change; she believes that you have some goodness in you, so she stays. You have children, so you have to think about them when you're about to go off. Think about all the consequences that come with beating your woman. Is it worth it? You've been down that road before, so you know where it ends. You know that you're going to apologize after you've finished beating on her, so just don't do it. I know it's hard when your blood starts boiling and your temper flares up, but you must find a way to control your anger. One of those times you're going to go off and accidentally kill her. You know you don't want that, so take heed to my advice and get help with your anger.

I'm not an anger management expert, but I'm an expert at living life. And I know that's no way to live your life. The world is bigger than you. Start taking into account the feelings of everyone around you. And so-called man, you know it too. Come to the other side where the real men and women are. I believe in you. I want you to be what God intended for you to be, a real man.

Start taking care of the children you fathered, you're not an animal. Animals fuck outside and have litters, and the male will disappear and go get another animal pregnant, and just keep it moving. Humans are supposed to stick around to take care of their offspring. Then you want to know why most of these women are so fucked up in the head. Most of them suffer from not having their father's around to show them how a man is supposed to treat a woman. So any treatment from a man

My Guide to Love & Romance

whether it be good or bad is sufficient. Most times it's these type of women who are generally the victims of malicious men.

And to the men who are in their children's life, providing for them and raising them into decent adults, I commend you all. You're the shining example of what a real man is. When I speak about what a real man is, it's you good brothers that I'm speaking about. It is because of you that there is some balance in the American family unit. Without the father in the equation, the family nucleus isn't whole. A family without both parents is dysfunctional by nature due to the fact that something is missing.

Here are some points I want to reiterate for any male reading this. These can be viewed as steps to becoming a real man if you're struggling to be one. Like I said, I'm not a man, but I know what a real man is.

- ☐ Honest and forthcoming
- ☐ Treats a woman like a Queen
- ☐ Sees himself as a king, and acts accordingly
- ☐ Always respectful
- ☐ Doesn't run from responsibility
- ☐ Stands firm on his principles

My Guide to Love & Romance

Listen to me very carefully, brothers. If you don't have a relationship with your children, it is never too late to build one. I know you may feel like they don't know you, and it's been so long since you've been in their lives. However, it's better for you to try than to give up on your own flesh and blood. It will only make the children better people, because every child needs a father.

So this one is for you, oh real man. You're a special and intricate element in society. If no one has ever told you, I want to take the time to say that Mama Jones appreciates you from the bottom of my heart. Keep up the good work. God Bless You All!

CHAPTER 20

"Step Your Game Up! No slackers allowed!"

Who are the fellows that really need this chapter? Fellows, if the title of this chapter makes you say to yourself, "She ain't lying. I need to step my game up," then this chapter is for you. If you don't work and you depend on your girl or your mother to take care of you, this is for you. If you work and make good money, but you have no swag or the slightest idea how to turn a woman on, this is for you. If you are slacking in any way when it comes to being a real man, this is for you. I'm going to be brutally honest with you fellows, so bear with me.

Everyone alive is worthy of a chance to get it right. We often refer to life as a game, but in this game most of us get more than three chances to win. I say most of us because some people don't get another chance to try again; that one mistake was fatal. So the fact that you're still here tells me that you

My Guide to Love & Romance

have another chance to step your game up and get it right. Like they say: "There is no better time than the present."

The Mama's Boy

Let's start with what I like to call **The Mama's Boy**, in honor of my namesake (Mama, pun intended). Some of you are like little babies, whining and throwing fits when you don't get your way. You haven't paid one bill in five years; your girl and your mother have carried you. I've never witnessed this amount of sissy ass men in my entire existence! They're everywhere. You see them hanging out on the block with their pants sagging. They are the ones that try to talk to every woman passing. They don't work a regular job; it's always something illegal, so they're in and out of jail. You have no backbone; you rely on a woman to take care of you and then you have the nerve to parade around calling yourself a man.

Here are some startling statistics that contribute to the Mama's Boy syndrome:

☐ According to the Census Bureau, 31% of young Black men live with their parents compared to only 11% of young Black women. A 20% point gap.

Mama Jones
My Guide to Love & Romance

- ☐ African Americans now constitute 1 million of the total 2.3 million people incarcerated in America.

- ☐ African Americans are incarcerated at nearly 6 times the rate of Whites.

- ☐ Blacks and Hispanics comprise 58% of all prisoners in 2008.

- ☐ One in three Black males born in America today can expect to spend time in prison.

- ☐ Unemployment for the general population is about 9.1%. It's at 16.2% for all Blacks, but for Black men it's 17.5%.

The Black man in America faces overwhelming adversity. With incarceration and unemployment so high, it's definitely difficult for you guys. No one is making excuses, but the numbers don't lie. There is an unequal playing field. However, this can be fixed with the right knowledge and a little action.

This is the advice I have for **The Mama's Boy.** I want you to look at your life and really be honest. You know you can do better than this. Be the man that your mother and your woman can be proud of. You and I both know you're not getting any younger. You have to change now. How much more jail time can you do? Do you think you can do another five-year bid? Then go right ahead and keep doing things illegal.

My Guide to Love & Romance

I don't think you want that, so here is what you're going to do. On Monday morning, you're going to get the newspaper (if you're not computer savvy), or go online and start looking for a job. Once you're hired and working eight hours a day, you'll notice a change in your behavior. You'll start feeling good about yourself. A day of honest work builds character in a man, and you'll begin to appreciate your hard earned money. Not to mention, idle time is the devil's playground, so you'll have less time to get into trouble and more time spent doing something productive.

It is a man's responsibility to be the backbone of a family and a relationship, so I expect you to step up and be what you are. God didn't design man to be weak. He made you strong. So you should at least match your woman's strength. How can you honestly call yourself a man when your woman works harder than you? When your woman gives you an allowance at the end of the week. Come on, son!

The funny thing about these types of men is that they really try to be the boss. I commend you for at least playing the role, but you're not quite there yet. You can be that man. Mama Jones believes in you even if you don't. I know for a fact that you can do it.

My Guide to Love & Romance

This is basically all you have to do to start the process of changing your life around for the better. The other stuff is easy, like paying some of the bills with your paycheck. Take your girl out on dates, buy her things, and be a gentleman. Life is too short to be living your life the way you've been living it. It's time to man-up!

Got Swag?

Now, on to what I like to call **'The Swag-less Man'**. This is the brother that has a good job, a career even, but has no swag. He doesn't know what a woman wants or how to deliver it; he is clueless to game. This type is oblivious to the fact that he is swag-less. He thinks he actually has style. Having money creates the illusion that you have swag, but money can't buy swag. However, you can be taught how to enter a little swag into your character.

Let me start by saying having swag is a state of mind. If you think cool, then you'll be cool. It sounds simple, but there is a little more to it. You have to believe it. You need the confidence to pull off the perfect swag. If you're not sure of yourself then your swag will come off like that, and you'll look corny instead of cool. You can't force it, it has to come off as natural even though it's not.

My Guide to Love & Romance

But when a man is confident, he exudes the aura of someone with impeccable swag. Ladies, watch out. There is nothing on God's green earth that can match a well-groomed man with swag. It's a weakness of most women, ain't it, ladies? A man with swag can step into a room and change the whole atmosphere. Now that's some powerful shit. Every woman in the room wants to know who this distinguished gentleman is.

The first step to acquiring swag is the belief in yourself, and then you have to execute every move as if it's calculated. Being that you're just beginning, you need to take your time with every step you take. You can mess up the whole theme by saying or doing something stupid. Make sure you think twice before saying anything. Once you've practiced being cool and you've got the basic hang of it, just continue to have confidence and belief in yourself and you'll be fine.

The Deadbeat

This next guy that needs to step his game all the way up is what we all like to call **The Deadbeat.** Yes, the classic Deadbeat. He's been around for a long time. It seems as

My Guide to Love & Romance

though the Black community is plagued with Deadbeats. Everywhere you turn there are single Black mothers struggling to take care of your children, you dead beat motherfucker. Excuse my French; it's just that these Deadbeats really get under my skin. I tried to keep the curse words at a minimum, but I had to let this one have it. I've always wanted to speak my mind about this subject, and what better time than the present.

I only have one piece of advice for the deadbeats of the world: Take care of your children! How can you consider yourself a real man when you've abandoned your offspring and left them for dead? You were man enough to make babies but not man enough to raise them. It takes a real man to raise children. It's a serious responsibility. I need all the deadbeats of the world to step up and be real men, not for your own self-gratification, but for the children!

The bottom line is that all of you men need to step your game up. It seems like a lot of the women of the world are doing much better than men nowadays. What I mean is, if it weren't for these strong women that hold it down, the family would be destroyed. At the rate that men are leaving these women, you would think that women would fall off. But no, we stand up and keep it moving. If the men of the world were

My Guide to Love & Romance

to stop for one second and analyze how strong their woman is, they'd have renewed respect for us. We hold it down, baby!

Fellows, pay attention to the details and you will see what you need to do. Some of you are so busy trying to run shit that you miss out on the little things. Smell the roses, admire a sunny day, and notice how green the grass is. Life is a beautiful thing, don't live it blind. Wake up and look around you. Be conscious, my brothers. Pay attention to your woman. She is your most precious jewel. When you treat your woman well, you'll notice your whole existence improve.

Last but not least, fellows, when the Love & Romance is dwindling and things seem to be coming to a close, here is what you have to do. Listen closely, you have to go back to that man you were when you first got together. You have to remember the way you were when you couldn't wait to see your girl, when she was always a pleasant thought on your mind. I know a lot has happened in the time you've been together. Forget about all that if it's not positive. Focus on the best of times and try to channel that energy. Once you've done that, now all you have to do is implement it into your relationship and witness it revitalize itself.

My Guide to Love & Romance

You have to keep it fresh, or it gets stale very fast. Everything on Earth has to be maintained. A well-manicured lawn doesn't look beautiful on its own. It's because the owner pays a landscaper to maintain it, so it will always appear lush and rich with green color. That is the same with a relationship, you have to play the landscaper and maintain the appearance of the relationship. It is always work when you're in a relationship. In the end it's always worth it when you have a loving partner. It takes two to make a thing go right!

Here is a recap of tips for the Mama's Boys to change your situation:

- ☐ Go online or get a newspaper and start looking for a job
- ☐ Once you're working, you'll start to feel good about yourself
- ☐ An honest day's work builds character
- ☐ Idle time is the devil's playground
- ☐ Appreciate hard earned money
- ☐ The bottom line is, when men out there begin to listen to us and start putting more effort into the relationship, then and only then will there be harmony between us. Women too, we have to listen to our man because he is shouting without using words. You just have to be conscious of his actions and you'll hear him. There is a

great divide between us that can be closed with a little guidance. Like I said, I'm no expert, but I know we have to strengthen our bond. Not only between man and woman, but between all humanity. I hope you all take heed and step your game up!

CHAPTER 21

"It's Not So Funny Now!
Ha, ha, ha—Karma's a bitch!"

This one goes out to all the womanizers of the world. Karma is a motherfucker! You've lived your whole life taking advantage of women. You've used them for your amusement and pleasure, and when you're done playing with us you want to toss us to the side like a broken toy. You take great pride in playing games with women; you brag about all your conquest as if they're spoils of war. You've gotten away with this behavior for years without a break. Now your teenage daughter is blossoming into a beautiful flower, and the wolves are lurking. You notice that she has the shape of her mother, very curvy. You do everything in your power to keep her sheltered because you know how men are dogs firsthand. It's not so funny when it's your own flesh and blood being targeted by men that are just like you.

My Guide to Love & Romance

Most womanizers don't think about things like this ever happening to them. They're so used to doing whatever to these women that they can't conceive of it hitting home one day. That's just how Karma works, it sneaks up on you when you least expect it. You won't see it coming, but boy when it hits home, it hits home, baby.

Let me tell you something. Most little girls are just like their fathers, just in a female version. All my daughters remind me of their fathers. So if you're a horny toad running around humping everything, what do you think your offspring will be? I hate to be the bearer of bad news, but most likely your daughter will be just like you.

It's funny to me because I've witnessed it firsthand with my own daughters. Remember, I have four girls and one boy, so I know all the little tricks. When they all came of age, their fathers were so over-protective of them that it was ridiculous. Men are very funny creatures, because they will play with women, but God forbid that a man ever plays with his little princess, then the world has come to an end. They can't take the idea that a man is going to treat his daughter the way he has treated women. Now it's not cool to treat a woman like

My Guide to Love & Romance

that, but it's too late—you've already set the karmic slate, and there's nothing you can do about it.

Let me tell you a little story. When Jelmoe first hit it big with his song "Ballin'", he couldn't help himself, women were all over him. Women were falling out; it was like something I've never seen before in my entire life. You would've thought this nigga was Michael Jackson or somebody. He was messing with at least twenty women at one time; my son was the poster child for womanizers.

I will never forget this night; I was in the crowd at one of Jelmoe's big shows in Harlem. I was looking fly as all outdoors. Mink on, and my hair and make-up was flawless. I was mingling when this tall, handsome young brother approached me. Of course, I checked him out. This brother had swag dripping out the wazoo! In case you haven't noticed, I look very young for my age, so I always get young guys trying to talk to me. At the time no one knew who I was; this was before the reality TV shows, so I was just another woman in the crowd.

So this fine ass brother was kicking it to me strong. I was feeling him too. I mean, he was all in my ear. He offered to buy me a drink, so I accepted. As the conversation continued, I was really digging this guy, so I let him dance up on me a

My Guide to Love & Romance

little. I was having a good old time until Jelmoe came out on the stage. He was talking on the mic and then his infamous "Ballin'" song came on, and I was jamming to it like everybody else. My new friend was behind me grinding on me. I felt his dick get hard on my ass. I thought, *I just might mess around with this guy.* That's when Jelmoe spotted me.

"Stop the fucking music!" Jelmoe ordered.

Everyone at the venue was stunned. They didn't know why he stopped the music, but I did. He was looking right at me and my new friend. "Oh, damn. It's about to be some shit up in here," I said loud enough for my friend to hear me. He got nervous because he could tell that Jelmoe was looking directly at us.

The whole crowd became silent. Everyone watched Jelmoe's eyes zero in on me. That's when Jelmoe jumped off the stage, stormed right up to me, picked me up and put me over his shoulder and carried me backstage right in front of at least 3,000 people. "Mommy, what the fuck are you doing out there? And who is that dude?" He looked at my new friend like he was going to kill him right where he stood. Jelmoe always has goons around him that can't wait to put in some work for him. I didn't want my new friend to get hurt, so I calmed Jelmoe down and he forgot all about him. Jelmoe got back on the stage and tore the house down with his performance.

I was about forty-seven at the time, and I never saw my new friend again after that. I would've gotten his number if Jelmoe wouldn't have cock-blocked. I guess it wasn't meant for him and me to be an item or else it would be. I believe everything happens for a reason. Let's just say that Jelmoe learned a very valuable lesson that night.

All the women my son took advantage of hit home for him in that one moment. He couldn't fathom the idea that his mother was with a man that resembled him. You have to understand, Jelmoe and I are more like brother and sister than mother and son. We're very close. He's my only son, so you know how that goes. Being that we're so close in age is the reason Jelmoe reacts the way he does when it comes to me. He jumped to the conclusion that I was being taken advantage of, so it wasn't so cool when it was someone close to him. It was all good when Jelmoe was doing it to someone else's daughter, sister, or mother. But the mere thought of it happening to someone close to him sent him over the edge. Not so funny now, is it?

My Guide to Love & Romance

That's the moral of this chapter. It's not so funny when someone is taking advantage of a female you Love. That's why men should always be considerate of the women they take advantage of. Women are human beings with delicate feelings. We're easily broken because we're so fragile. If all the players of the world were to take into consideration that these women have delicate feelings and emotions like their loved ones, they probably wouldn't do the shit anymore!

Jelmoe has always been very protective of me. He couldn't take the thought of his mother becoming a victim of a womanizer. It has only gotten worse since the reality TV fame. OMG! Jelmoe loses his mind if I go anywhere without my security. I can't go to do my radio and TV interviews, make VIP appearances, or go anywhere without the security team Jelmoe provided for me. At first it made me feel special, but a girl has to have her privacy without some goon all up in my business.

I know Jelmoe's intentions are golden, so I just listen to him as if he's the parent. I'm only seventeen years older than Jelmoe, so we're pretty close in age. Sometimes Jelmoe thinks he's my father the way he orders me around, but I know it's

My Guide to Love & Romance

just his way of being protective. Like he always says, "I only have one mother."

Did you know I now have stalkers since the *Love & Hip Hop* show was a success? Yes, and let me tell you something. These male groupies are far worse than female groupies. A male groupie can stalk your ass right into a grave because they're crazy as hell. So Jelmoe has good reason to be overprotective, because there are some crazies out there. He knows all too well about stalkers. Jelmoe has had more than his fair share of them, trust me.

I've been stalked by fans, but this one time it got a little serious. It was a fan of *Love & Hip Hop* that used to hit me up on Twitter and Facebook. He started making disturbing comments about what he was going to do to me if he ever sees me. It was pretty creepy stuff. It never got to the point where I had to call the cops to get a restraining order; it was just online. But I still feared for my life. One piece of advice I have for anyone being stalked is: Watch out for anyone that looks suspicious or spends too much time on your social media pages. Unfriend them and report them to Facebook or any other social media outlet.

Listen, I know it's fun to have three or more women at one time catering to your male ego. You can have them all; you manage the time spent with each one equally. But there comes a time when you have to grow up and fly right. You have kids now, so you have to show them the right way. You can't show your sons that it's cool to have all these women. You know you don't want him to grow up like that. And what about your daughters? Do you want them to grow up thinking it's okay to have multiple relationships at one time? Of course not, you'd lose your mind if your daughters were to mirror your activity.

It's definitely an addiction, especially if a man has been doing it since he was a teen. But there is help. Men, don't be afraid to see a psychologist about your behavior. You may not see it, but your behavior is a mental disorder. That's right. Men who womanize suffer from all sorts of abandonment and self-image issues. Why else would someone get pleasure from being sadistic? This is a serious problem that has been swept under the rug and summed up as just something that men do. It's far from just a characteristic of men; this is a full-fledged mental disorder. And just like all the other disorders, this one progresses with time and activity. Some of these men become sociopaths because their behaviors progress.

These types of men become incessant womanizers. They can't help themselves. I have men as best friends that have

My Guide to Love & Romance

confided in me that they want to stop cheating but they can't. One of my male friends is in Love with his girlfriend, but he just can't stop being with other women. He says sometimes it's the women that won't stop even after he informed them he was in a committed relationship. They still pursued a sexual relationship with him. That's like a recovering crack head being constantly approached by drug dealers that want to give him crack for free. Of course he's going to take it; he has an addiction.

And some of you women are to blame for some of this treacherous behavior because you're trifling. You're a woman, so you know what it feels like to be cheated on, but you do it anyway. You know he doesn't Love you, but you humiliate yourself, and ultimately the whole female species when you mess with a married man. You're enabling him to continue this vicious cycle. But this part of the book is dedicated to the men; I'll get back to you later.

All of us, men and women alike, need to be mindful of one another. That's what is really wrong with the world; we've lost our sense of oneness. Everyone is running around going for themselves so much that we forget about our fellow man/woman. We've lost our sense of community, our sense of

My Guide to Love & Romance

compassion for humanity itself. It can definitely be restored, but it'll take a lot of hard work from everyone.

I hate to sound preachy, but I sincerely believe in the things I'm saying. I may not be highly educated, but I do know the survival of the human race requires togetherness. We need each other to survive. Together we can change this negative world we live in. Together we can reinstate the process of Love to the world. The world is suffering from a lack of Love and understanding.

I'm not going to put all the blame on the men. I'm merely talking to you guys because this part of the book is strictly for you. Fellows, if you fit the description of the character in this chapter, it's okay. I'm not judging you. Hell, I would probably do what you do if I were a man. Society says it's acceptable for men to have many women, so you see nothing immoral about your conduct. Believe me, I understand, but you know that you can't go on living like this. You know that you're hurting these women deeply when you play with their emotions. And you know that each and every time you hurt a woman, you also get hurt at the end of the day. You can pretend you don't care, but deep down inside you're human and you have feelings and emotions just like the women you

My Guide to Love & Romance

injure. You can front like you don't care when she is crying her heart out to you in an attempt to stop the pain. You're good at pretending not to care, but we all know what the truth is. Also, remember that womanizers fall into the category of sex-addicts because the cheating is really about sex. That's just something for you to think about.

Here are some interesting tips for women dealing with a womanizer, and for men that fall into the category of womanizer/sex-addict:

- ☐ Realize that womanizing is an addiction. It needs to be defined and treated as such.
- ☐ The womanizer is the only person who can decide to alter his ways and seek the help he needs.
- ☐ A womanizer's behavior is no reflection on his woman's capacity as a partner.
- ☐ Denial, rationalizing, excuses and forgiveness do not help bring about recovery.
- ☐ Both partners must understand the nature of the addiction and commit to dealing with it.
- ☐ Women must safeguard their own well-being, which at times require separating from the womanizer.
- ☐ Recovery is possible. It takes awareness, time, energy, money and commitment.

My Guide to Love & Romance

Here are some places where you can go to get help if you suffer from womanizing/sexual addiction:

1. Recovery Ranch—Provides relationship and sex recovery treatment programs. (recoveryranch.com).

2. Sexual Recovery Institute—Provides sexual addiction screening tests for men and women. (sexualrecovery.com).

3. Sex Addict Treatment Center—Specializes in porn addiction rehabilitation. (saa-recovery.org)

Until next time, Ciao!

CHAPTER 22

"Boyz Will be Boyz!
Be a leader!"

At the end of the day, when it's all said and done, the fact remains, Boyz will be Boyz. And that's what I understand most of all, just like women will be women. Although it sounds like I'm male bashing at times, I'm really not. I'm just pointing out some of the things that will make Love & Romance enjoyable. Yes, I do want men to take my words seriously, but make no mistakes about it, I Love you guys. That's the beauty of this thing called life. We all just want to live, be happy, and have fun. Women wouldn't Love men if they didn't do some of the things they do, even some of the bad things. We Love you unconditionally, but that doesn't mean we have to like all of your ways.

My Guide to Love & Romance

Tips to the Guys:

With that being said, I would like to bring something to your attention. Guys, just be a little mindful of your lady. I mean, don't leave your clothes lying around just because you know your lady will pick up after you. Try to be neater than you've been. Another thing, please start putting the damn toilet seat up when you urinate. Not only is it disgusting getting piss all over the toilet seat, it's inconsiderate. I know you guys can be better. It's all about your upbringing, but a lot of the negative things you do are sanctioned by society. Society says it's okay for you to have multiple women. There is a double standard when it comes to what a man can do. No matter how liberated women have become, being promiscuous is not a good look. She'll be called the biggest whore on the planet.

I have four grandsons, and right before the printing of this book I became a proud great grandmother. I'm teaching all my grandsons how to be distinguished gentlemen at an early age. They're all extremely polite and their manners are impeccable. The little ones are going to be perfect boyfriends when they get older because they'll have the utmost respect for women.

My Guide to Love & Romance

Of course, they're still young men, however, this is a crucial stage in their life. What they've learned will stick with them for the rest of their existence, and I wanted respect to be near the top of the list.

Respect is the one element missing from this generation's moral compass. Once men regain the respect for women, things in Love land will be all good again.

I hate to keep harping on the same topic, but rap music heavily promotes disrespect of women. And because of it, young Black men in general are more disrespectful. You have to remember, before the creation of this gangster rap, there was only R&B, Soul, and Disco in the Black community. All of those genres never put women down. In fact, it did the opposite. It made us feel beautiful and wanted. Rap didn't singlehandedly turn our young men into heartless womanizers. I blame society as well, because it tells our young men that it's okay to be a womanizer. I remember watching *Happy Days* and seeing Arthur Fonzarelli be admired for always having two or three women on his arm (Some of you are too young to remember *Happy Days*). Then you have all these reality TV shows with men dating twenty women, like a damn harem or something. Makes me sick how they promote womanizing on TV. But I didn't make the rules, society did.

My Guide to Love & Romance

Even so, I have confidence that there are enough good men out there to tip the scales on the bad ones. I know it seems like all is lost, but with a little communication and education, we can save the world. I know that sounds like a reoccurring theme in this guide. Sometimes repetition is good. Especially, when it's something as serious as saving the world.

I'm calling on you good men to step up and show the young brothers how to be good men. They are lacking in good examples, so they're taking manhood classes from the bad guys. You see it everywhere you go. That's why the youth turn to the streets and gangs because that's the only classroom left. Their street teachers are giving them the wrong life lessons, so we end up with disrespectful, no-good men. A woman can only teach a boy but so much before he's going to need a real man to show him how to be a man. That's a major problem in the hood. There aren't enough good men out there mentoring. If we had more good men out there teaching these young brothers, the world would be a better place.

Yes, there are some good men out there. I happen to know a few. One of my close friends is a real good man. He takes care of his family; he sacrificed so he could send his children to college. He taught them to be respectful young men, and they are just like their father. I use my friend as a shining example whenever I need one. He is dedicated to his family and his community and he bonds with other like-minded men. A handful of these brothers can teach an army of young males how to be real men.

It's very important that this message gets out there to all the good men so they can band together to make a change. I know there are organizations set up just for the type of male bonding I'm speaking of. If you don't have a male support group in your community, create one. Be the leader, you don't have to wait for someone to lead you. Take a stand! I just think we need to do more.

I'm out there in every city across America. I see all the young men and women desperately seeking guidance from anywhere. They talk to Mama Jones because they view me as someone worthy to give sound advice. I know exactly why the youth tend to gravitate toward me. I know it has something to do with the show and my son, but I have a responsibility to guide them in the right way. I am Mama Jones, Hip Hop's favorite mother, so I guess it's my responsibility to enlighten the youth growing up in this young musical genre. That's why so many young people Love Mama Jones. I'm here for you all.

My Guide to Love & Romance

My main concern isn't the here and now; I'm more worried about the future. What is this world coming to? A scary end, that's what. I think we're living in the last days. Just look around you. Everyone is going for self; no one cares about their fellow man. I have grandkids that will be here twenty to thirty years from now. The way it looks, the world is going to be a war zone filled with evil. We have to learn to be as ONE; that's the only way for us to really transform the world into the beautiful paradise that God intended this to be.

As long as I'm alive I will fight you, Satan! God is with me and His power is unlimited! You will not win, even if it seems that you have everything locked down. God will defeat you! There is no doubt in my mind that I'm here to fight for what is right. I wasn't blessed for nothing. I know exactly what I have to do, and I'm doing it. This is as serious as cancer, I know all too well how serious cancer is. The world is on the brink of extinction if we don't act now! Everyone make a stand for God.

This will conclude Part V. This has been enlightening to say the least because it was a chance for me to get a lot of stuff off my chest. I know it's hard for some men to take advice from a woman, but this is more than advice. It's a message from the Almighty God himself. He is the one that allowed this book to happen; it's for Him. Lord knows the world is in need of something positive. This guide is more like divine inspiration because I didn't choose to write books, writing books chose me. When the idea came to me, I knew exactly what it was. "God wants me to do this," I said to myself.

Truly, it was a pleasure speaking with you guys. I hope you've found some wisdom in my words, and most of all, I hope you take heed and take action. Without action there is no progress, and that's what this is all about, progress. I thank you for your time and energy.

I'm going to repeat some action steps that I want you to keep in mind:

- ☐ Guys, be mindful of your lady and try to be a little neater. Pick up after yourself.
- ☐ Have more respect for your woman.
- ☐ Mentor younger men to be respectful gentlemen.
- ☐ Be a leader! Get involved in the community.
- ☐ Take a stand!

God Bless. Ciao!

The

Conclusion

Mama Jones
My Guide to Love & Romance

CHAPTER 23

"Finding Love
When you finally find your soul mate, you'll know it's
powerful love."

Guess what? You made it! You made it through my guide. Now I have to let you in on a few secrets. The Love that you were looking for was right in front of your face the whole time. It was you! You were looking for yourself. The illusion is that you thought this was about you finding Love outside of yourself. When the whole time it was you that you needed to find and fall in Love with. You needed to find the one true Love that really matters, the Love of Self.

There is no other Love in the world that will have a profound effect on you like the Love of Self. Once you have realized this fact, then your soul mate will find you as well. The connection will be so strong that it will overwhelm you at times. It is a powerful Love. It's the same Love that created the whole universe! It is the heartbeat of the cosmos that is in unison with you and your newfound Love.

There is no other force that exists in the Universe that can match the power of true Love. We are all connected through the force of Love because God is Love and he created us all from that Love. So that means that we are pure Love in a physical form. We were created out of Love, to Love, because that is our sole purpose in this life. To Love life is to really live it. When you embrace the pure Love of all things, then you transcend to that highest level of existence while on earth. Your connection to the Universe and God is through the element of pure Love. To embrace God is to embrace Love and vice versa.

Don't be afraid to go as deep as this guide will take you. This is all about you coming to the realization of the Self. When we become aware of that energy that exists within us and awaken to the truth, is when our eyes are open. We see life through correct vision. This whole world is an illusion because NOTHING in it is as it REALLY is, only how it appears to be to the naked eye. On the outside, you see one thing when everything that exists is more than it seems. For instance, look at me. I'm a fifty-four-year-old Black woman

My Guide to Love & Romance

from Aruba, who grew up in Harlem and raised five kids. Guess what? That is only what you are designed to see. You can't see the energy that makes me a living, breathing being. It has no shape, no color. It's formless just like the energy in everything. So what am I? I am Love! In the physical form, and so are you. Without Love you wouldn't exist, and without God you wouldn't exist. Remember, God is Love! They are one and the same.

We have to understand that this world is a stage. We are all characters in a play called *"Life"*. We are all playing our designated part, which becomes who we are. You know, I'm Nancy Jones from Harlem, etc. However, there is only one actor playing all the parts. That actor is God. HE is always present. HE is also the director and the scriptwriter. He knows exactly what's going to happen before it takes place because he wrote the script. At the end of the day, when it's all said and done and the show is over, God takes a bow for his stellar performance. HE is the all knower, the best planner, so this thing called Life is HIS design.

So how does it feel to finally know the truth? You might not understand it yet; there is still more to learn. Nevertheless, you have the directions to that glorious destination. It's up to you to put in the work to get there. I'm sure if you've read this guide you'll be okay for the rest of the ride. It's not what you know; it's what you do with your knowledge that really counts. I am a firm believer that everything happens for a reason. You're reading this wonderful guide for a divine purpose. God has intended for your eyes to be wide open, for your candle to be lit. The lights are on now.

Still, there is another force at work. It's a dark force that wants to keep our candles from being lit inside. Satan's minions want us to remain in darkness because that is how they stay in power. This dark force uses technology like magic. They're able to deceive the masses in the blink of an eye without them being the slightest bit aware of what's really going on. This dark force is bent on enslaving the minds of every living soul that exists. The reason the masses are not aware of the Self is because it was designed that way. Because they do not want to awaken *The Sleeping Giant*. Once we are all awakened, then the evil doers' reign is over.

The only power they have is defining *Reality*. Now, what does Mama Jones mean by *Defining Reality?* Well, let me give you a quote from Dr. Leonard Jeffries, professor of African American Studies at City College in New York.

My Guide to Love & Romance

"Power is the ability to define reality, and have others respond to it as if it were their own."

I'm on *reality TV,* which isn't reality at all. It should've been called *Bogus TV, or Phony TV.* I say that because they named it "reality" to make you believe that it's real, when it's not. A friend of mine asked me one day, "Are the reality TV shows scripted?" They are, and they are not—let me explain. They'll have us show up to the location and script a meeting or something, the rest is improvisation. But let me tell you something, them fights are fucking real! You better duck, because them chicks be throwing bottles and shit be crazy!

The *Powers-that-be* have been defining reality for the masses for hundreds of years. They keep us from the truth that we are all ONE, because we all stem from the same source, which is God. If they can make us think we are all different, then they can take us away from the oneness that we need to defeat their wicked plan for world domination.

They are against anything righteous and Godly. They are anti-God and seek to destroy Love. That's the real reason there is so much hate in the world, because they promote it purposely. There could be peace on the Earth, but they are anti-peace. That's why there is so much war. Anything that has to do with the light of the truth and Love, which is God, they are opposed to. They want to keep us all in the dark.

It's too late for that now, isn't it? If you made it this far into this work, you are already sparked by the truth, which is the light. There is a Spiritual War going on where Satan wants to win your soul. He doesn't want you to embrace the beautiful messages of Love and Unity that are in this book. He knows once it reaches the masses, he will lose the war. He is winning the battle, but as sure as my name is Mama Jones—Satan will be defeated by God.

In fact, Satan wants to launch a world war like the world has never seen before. They've been stock piling missiles prepared to blow up half of this Earth. Everything is in place for their wicked plan of world destruction. What he doesn't know is that God has a plan too. And remember, God is the best of planners. It could seem as though Satan is right at the brink of winning, and then out of nowhere God will strike and thwart everything he is trying to do.

I don't want to get sidetracked. My spirit wanted me to throw that out there. Now, back to you, my new friend in the Truth. Now, I want you to do Mama Jones a favor. Go out into the world with your new glow, and radiate the light of the truth. Learn to light other inner candles, because people are going to gravitate toward you. It's like a moth to a flame; your inner glow is visible on a spiritual plane. Don't freak out when people look at you funny. It's just that your light is amazing to the soul that isn't lit. The soul yearns to be lit, so that it can dwell in the light of truth. Who wants to be in the dark their whole life? No one. Everyone wants to know the truth, to know that there is a force trying to KEEP you in the dark. Once the light is lit, there is no turning it off. It is an eternal flame that can't be extinguished. Satan knows this, so his main concern is to stop the light from illuminating everywhere, lighting up every inner candle that exists. It's happening as we speak. Whose side are you on?

Rejoice in your newfound Love of Self. Your life will be on autopilot, just sit back while God does the driving. All you have to do now is relax your mind and live in the moment of the Truth. I'm happy for you, because I know if you made it this far then you are really on your way. I'm so proud of you and so is God, for this is his work like I said before. I'm just the messenger. God is the message. Love is the goal. Congratulations. You have reached the ultimate destination, which is Truth.

Mama Jones
My Guide to Love & Romance

Here are a few steps toward loving yourself:

1. Vision an inner light of peace and focus on it.
2. Once you can focus on it, imagine the light becoming brighter.
3. Let it become brighter until you become the light.
4. Understand that you are the light, and the light is Love.
5. Shine!

This is a serious occasion for anyone who is reading this. We are all connected by the truth I manifest. We must learn to Love again. We've fallen from the perch of our spiritual Father's bosom. We must remember why we're here. It's not to kill, rape, steal or hate; it's to Love unconditionally. I'm confident that you will tell a friend about this great work.

Tell the truth. I bet you thought this was going to be some bullshit, because they paint me as a crazy lady on so-called reality TV. It's okay, I would've thought the same. Actually, I think that when I see the footage of me going off on the reality TV show, too. That's all for the ratings. I'm really not like that. I'm far from that as you can attest from reading my guide. I'm a true child of God, a soldier in his righteous army. I'm only 5-feet 2-inches tall and 100 pounds soaking wet, but I bet you this: I cannot be defeated! Because God has my back! Satan, you have a problem, and her name is Mama Jones!

I'm a giving, loving person who is all about family. Even till this day I have relatives that know they can ask me for anything and I'll give it to them if I have it. Now that I'm a grandmother, it's all about them. All of my kids are grown, so I have great joy in seeing my grandchildren grow up. I might be a little 'psychotic', but overall I have a good heart. I have found the Love inside of me.

Finding Love is the objective of this whole book. Now that we have come to the point of no return, are you ready to Love? I mean, *really* ready to Love unconditionally. Everything and everyone, no matter what their race or gender. That's what I'm talking about! Let's show them who the real boss is, because Love will always prevail. Once again, congratulations on finding Love.

Mama Jones
My Guide to Love & Romance

CHAPTER 24

"Creating Romance
Romance is the glue that holds Love together."

N ow that we have found Love and have a pretty good understanding of what Love really is, the job isn't over. The new problem is creating Romance. We've established in chapter 3 that you can't have Romance without Love. Romance is the glue that holds Love together. So knowing this, how do you create Romance? I mean, can you actually create Romance? Of course we can. Allow Mama Jones to show you something.

Once true Love is in place, from both parties, then and only then can you reach the pinnacle of Romance. I have to be honest with you. You cannot create any real Romance until both parties are truly in Love with each other. I mean that Love-that-I've-been- describing-in-this-book kind of Love. That deep, unconditional, real Love. If you have surface Love, then you will have surface Romance, which isn't Romance at

My Guide to Love & Romance

all. It's the illusion of Romance, which is lust. In order to create that pure Romance, you also have to be spontaneous and adventurous. Romance is forever evolving in a loving relationship because you can't do the same things over and over. What you think is romantic, becomes some corny shit out of a Cracker Jack Box.

When you're in Love, you will find yourself being naturally romantic. Romance isn't sex or lust. It's the silence while caressing your mate. Inside that silence is the origin of Romance. The silence represents a moment in time that can't be measured with a clock. The silence is that space where Love comes from. The silence isn't really silence at all because it screams romantic chants to your spirit that you feel on a deep inner level. It's the foundation for Love songs and great poems. It's an endless well from which all things good and pure spring from. It's a deep passion for Love that creates true Romance.

I'm going to share some powerful steps on how to use the power of silence in Romance:

- ☐ Meditate on nothing but silence
- ☐ Still your mind; try to stop the mind from thinking

My Guide to Love & Romance

☐ Understand that the silence isn't really silence at all. It's a zone between space and time

☐ Share the experience with your Lover to reach new heights of Love and understanding one another

This is the highest level of Romance. These points are an introduction to foreplay with the mind. To me foreplay is the sexiest, most romantic thing you can do that doesn't require sex itself. Silence is foreplay, ladies and gentlemen!

If you made it this far in this guide then you've scratched the surface of that deep inner Love that I speak about. Which means you are ready to create some Romance in your relationship. With time and practice will come that deeper understanding of everything I'm manifesting. Do you think it took me reading one book, one time, to come to this conclusion? Of course not. To be honest, I didn't come into this understanding until my late 40's. I've always had some wisdom because I've always had wise people around me to guide me. So in turn, I'm giving it back. That's how wisdom works. When you give it away, you actually strengthen it in yourself simultaneously, lighting another candle.

I have to let you in on another little secret about Romance. Romance is a state of mind triggered by being in real Love. The bottom line is that once you have figured out what real

My Guide to Love & Romance

Love is, you instinctively become a romantic. Your passion about everything increases ten-fold. You will be what some like to call a 'Hopeless Romantic'. You can't turn it off just like you can't turn off Love once you understand it.

I Love the Romance of it all. Romance is what makes you stay in Love with that person of your affection. You have to understand, Romance is just as potent as Love once you comprehend it on a deeper level. If God is Love, then He is having a romantic relationship with the life of the living. He loves us romantically, or else He would just destroy us for not following his commandments. Lord knows that we have fallen from his grace, but He still loves us unconditionally. God's expression is Romance because His Love is so pure.

I don't want to make this sound like a religious book because it's not. It's a highly spiritual book. I have to speak about God because it's the truth that without God there is no Love. It doesn't matter what religion you are, spirituality is Universal. It transcends the concept of a man-made religion. I just wanted to clarify that because I'm mentioning God quite a bit in this work. It's okay, because it's the absolute truth.

We're creating Romance as we speak, because the vibrations of the words are directly connected to my passion.

Mama Jones
My Guide to Love & Romance

Speaking to people about the truth has always been one of my passions. Passion and Romance are one and the same because I have to be romantically involved in what I do to Love it. We can't limit Romance to relationships. You have to have a Romance with the truth. You have to have a Romance with life, and last but not least with God.

The Romance of life is like a dance to the tune of a beautifully assembled orchestra, like on *Dancing with the Stars*. I've always wanted to be on *Dancing with the Stars* because I Love to dance. I can dance all night long, baby, always could. There is something about dancing that is magical to me, to be able to be in sync with the rhythm. The same way that Love is in sync with Romance. They are in complete unison, dancing to the tune of a Universal rhythm. Maybe after this book is published I can get auditioned for *Dancing with the Stars*. Who knows? Anything is possible.

Did you know that with Love & Romance present in your life that you attract blessings? It's so true; I'm a witness to this fact. I wouldn't tell you a lie. Ever since I've been on this spiritual path I've been receiving blessing after blessing. I got rid of all the bad influences, and I got blessed to be on *Love & Hip Hop*, the first season. While I was doing the show, I got approached to do all these other things, like, start my own clothing line called Psychotic, which started out as a diss from my son's fiancée. She called me 'psychotic' on the show, and I took it and made it into an empire. The popularity of the song allows me to tour around the world, and I've created a clothing line of that same brand name, and secured a vodka deal! From there I started my own perfume line called Pum-Kash. I also have Pum-Kash candles, lip-gloss, and Papa 2 Che, which is my men's cologne line. And last but not least, this book. Now, if that's not a lot of blessings I don't know what a blessing is! I thank the Almighty God for every one of them. And I just keep on getting blessed. Still, it is all due to Love, my Love for God and life. I can't tell you how much I Love the Romance of living life. Enough to sit down and write this guide for the world. This has been a journey within itself that is far from over. I plan to keep on writing more books. This is just the beginning. I've been blessed with the wisdom, and while I have the life in me to do it, I'm going to keep on grinding, baby.

Did you know the positive energy of Love will keep you energized? I'm up all day, running around doing interviews and VIP parties at night, just to wake up and do it all again. And I'm fifty-four years old. I'm here to tell you it's because

My Guide to Love & Romance

of my positive outlook on life; it creates positive energy. Not only that, but I don't get sick, and I think I look pretty damn good for fifty-four, thank you. I'll say it again. It's because of the romantic Love affair I have with life and God.

I can go on for days telling you the positive ramifications when embracing Love & Romance and applying it to your everyday existence. Not only does it enhance your life, but it touches everyone in your circumference. People are always gravitating to me and I know why. It's not only because of the reality TV show; it's something deeper than that. I sincerely Love every one of God's creations, wholeheartedly and unconditionally. The reason people Love Mama Jones is because Mama Jones loves the people.

Do Mama Jones a big favor. I know I've asked for a few so far, but it's not for me, it's for you. Promise me that you will live your life from this day forward with the Romantic Love that I'm prescribing in this guide.

Can you do that for Mama Jones? I'd appreciate it very much if you would. If you do this one thing for me, I promise you blessings of health and good fortune. I'm no prophet, but I know positive vibrations work similar to a boomerang; they come back to you in the form of blessings. When you're a good person and you think positive thoughts, along with being

My Guide to Love & Romance

genuinely kind to others, you create positive karma that places your life-force energy in a harmonious balance. That balance creates happiness within, which ultimately manifests on the outside. People will always notice your light because it's positive.

There are many benefits to thinking Positive. I'm talking about not judging, or getting violent, even when someone is being nasty to you. Random acts of charity and kindness are excellent ways to practice living a positive life. Get in tune with nature, go on long walks through a forest, or if you live near the ocean, visit it just to meditate and speak to God.

Practice being conscious of the Love for everyone and everything. Have a romantic relationship with living life, with Love as the core belief, and watch your being transform right in front of your eyes.

What usually works for me is meditating and realizing that I am alive, living with a purpose. Like I said, my main purpose in life now is to take care of my grandbabies. Yours may be your career. Whatever it is, get romantically involved with it and think positive. Learn what works for you and customize your own positive program.

Mama Jones
My Guide to Love & Romance

This is not a gimmick, or one of those false promises that preachers make to their flock to get more money in the collection plate. I'm guaranteeing you a life of peace and harmony if you follow all of my instructions. I know I sound preachy sometimes, but you get what I'm saying. That's the most important thing.

I hope you learned a thing or two about Romance in this chapter. Romance is what you make it once you've figured out the components of Love. I don't have to keep telling you. I know you got it from here. Statistics show that people who have been in Love for long periods of time live happier and healthier lives. The same way a break-up can cause extreme pain, a great bond can cause extreme happiness. Enjoy life and live it to the fullest, now that you have a solid understanding of Love & Romance.

Mama Jones
My Guide to Love & Romance

CHAPTER 25

"What Does it All Mean?
Your candle is eternally lit once you're spiritually
awake."

You know Mama Jones got a lot of Love for you. This book will definitely build a bridge to a better understanding and better communication, not only in relationships, but with humanity as a whole. This book will help maintain an honest and respectful dialogue between men and women. Book clubs can use it to discuss building better relationships. I'm confident that God has his hands in this guide. That's why I chose to call it a guide because I want to lead people in the right direction. I want to show Satan that God has soldiers here fighting the good fight too.

So, what does it all mean? That's a good question. I know I've written enough to make you crossed eyed by now. Nevertheless, I've spoken about communication, and I've

My Guide to Love & Romance

given you my list of do's and don'ts, rights and wrongs, good and bad. DO YOU FEEL LIKE YOU'VE ACCOMPLISHED ANYTHING? I'm here to say, you're damn right you've accomplished something by reading my guide. This is much more than meets the eye; this is a spiritual awakening, a candle lighting so to speak, because now your candle is eternally lit! That's only if it wasn't lit prior to you completing this guide. If so, I only enhanced the flame. This is about Love & Romance, but halfway through the guide you understand the connection between Love of Self and Love for everyone as a whole because we are all ONE. We all stem from ONE SOURCE, which is GOD!

This has been quite a journey for me as well, more so for me because it gave me a chance to vent and also clean out some things in my mental closet. You know you have to do that sometimes, clean out your mental closet, because you don't want it getting too cluttered in there. But this was more than just that, it was also a spiritual progression as well. I feel more connected to the world at large due to this wonderful guide on Love & Romance. I cannot express how amazing I feel to be blessed enough to have God use little old me to get his message of Love out to the world! Like I keep saying, this is God's work, not mine, because it was in His plans. I put

My Guide to Love & Romance

everything in His hands and this is what He has manifested in my life. I'm so grateful to God for everything that He has done for me, not just the fame and money, but the health and well-being of my children and myself, along with the continued blessings.

I feel like this guide is an extension of those blessings from God through me to all those that read this work. There is immense spiritual energy attached to this work, so much that anyone that completes it is automatically blessed by God Almighty. This is not a hoax or an attempt to win your favor. I'm not a priest or any member of the clergy. I'm a child of God, just doing what my Father instructs me to do. There is no hocus pocus, no smoke and mirrors, only the truth, which is that God allows everything to happen, or else it wouldn't take place.

There have been a lot of negative things that have taken place in the last twenty years or so that have ripped holes in the moral fabric of the world. I couldn't believe what happened with Trayvon Martin! I thought for sure they would find Zimmerman guilty. My condolences go out to his family. I have five grandchildren that are young Black men just like Trayvon; it could've easily been one of them. My heart also

My Guide to Love & Romance

goes out to those three young women that were held captive for eleven years in Ohio. They were repeatedly raped and beaten, but they survived. Thank God. Then a seventy-seven-year-old man killed a thirteen-year-old child right in front of his mother! And the whole thing was caught on video. I can go on for days about all the madness going on in the world today. Surely, these tragic stories solidify my claim that the world is lacking in love.

All we need is Love; it's as simple as that. That's what God wants us all to understand, the Oneness of a human family that loves one another like the true brothers and sisters that we are. When we achieve that Unconditional Love for the human family that God wants us to have, then this will be a heaven on Earth. No more wars, famine, murders, molestations, or abuse of any kind. It will be a world where the color of your skin or the customs and beliefs of your religion won't cloud the one simple fact: we are all God's children. Not just one group of people, or the White ones or Black ones, everyone. Together we make up the human family, ONE human family.

Romance is the expression of this Unconditional Love that I speak of. When we see ourselves as extended family, then we will treat our significant others with the utmost respect that we deserve, creating the greatest romantic atmosphere you can

My Guide to Love & Romance

imagine. For example, I'm a Black woman. I got Love for everybody, no matter your race or ethnicity. We may have different colors and cultures, but we all bleed the same human blood. In fact, when a White man or Black man needs a blood transfusion, they don't care what color the donor is, just give him or her the blood, right? Romance is like the child of Love because there is no Romance without Love. Like I said before, there can be lust but not Romance.

I want people to keep this book as a life-guide. Something to pick up every now and then and learn a lesson from. This is a true guide, a path to the inner peace you seek. I want you to learn how to go to that space at will and dwell in the bliss of life. I want you to have a romantic affair with your man or woman on a level that will rival heaven itself. I want all races and ethnicities to Love one another like sister and brother, without prejudice. I want the world to understand that we are all ONE!

I have a few questions for the ladies before we wrap this up:
1. Is your man serious about a commitment?
2. Are you afraid to give your man an ultimatum?

My Guide to Love & Romance

3. Are you ready for a commitment?

4. If you catch your man cheating, do you give him another chance?

5. How many chances is too many?

6. Where do you draw the line?

7. Does your man REALLY Love you?

8. Do you REALLY Love your man?

9. Do you have a better understanding of Love & Romance after reading this book?

10. Do you feel like you have a better concept of life in general after reading this book?

Now I have a few questions for the fellows:

1. Did you learn anything about women from reading this guide?

2. Do you have a better understanding of yourself as a man after reading this guide?

3. Are you ready for a commitment with one woman?

4. Do you ever see yourself married?

5. Are you ready to mentor young boys to help them become young men?

My Guide to Love & Romance

6. If you are a womanizer as defined in this guide, are you willing to get the proper help with your sexual addiction?

7. If you are abusive to women, are you willing to get the help you need to address it?

8. If you have been an absent father, will you consider being in your child's life?

9. If you are a Mama's Boy, are you ready to leave the nest?

10. Are you ready to change the world for the better?

Ladies and gents, I want you to ponder on your answers before you give them. Contemplate on truth, because this test is between you and you. I'm never going to know the answers to these questions, so be totally honest. Besides, if you can't be honest with yourself then who can you be honest with?

Ultimately, we all just want our mate to Love us enough to want to do romantic things for us. It's what drives the vehicle of Love, and if you have a rider, he or she will ride until the wheels fall off. That's what it's all about, Love & Romance!

My final advice for the ladies: Find that FEMININE POWER and use it for the greater good of all humanity. Be whatever you want to be. Don't let anybody stop you from being the best. There were haters in my life that always told me I wouldn't be shit, and I proved them wrong. And so can you!

Finding the Love & Romance you seek is a matter of taking the steps to get in tune with yourself enough for it to happen. When you connect with that FEMININE POWER I speak of, you will not only find Love & Romance, but you'll find purpose. Stop being catty with one another and stick together on issues that matter. Like women's rights and breast cancer awareness, those are issues that we need to be discussing with the youth. Ladies, let's all step up and be the Queens we were meant to be!

Fellows, this is not just a man's world. It's a world for all living things. Let a man go into the ocean and tell a whale that it's a man's world. Or go tell that to a lion without a gun or any weapon. Understand that your woman is your equal opposite and she should be treated as such. Stop disrespecting women! Young man, your mother would be ashamed of you if she saw how you carry on in the streets, calling these women 'hos and bitches. You wouldn't like for any man to call your mother those names, so don't call any woman those names. It's not hard to be a gentlemen to the ladies. Try it, you may see that you get more bees with honey, if you catch my drift. When we all realize that we all have a role that is equally important, then and only then will this world be transformed into a Utopia.

I've learned a whole lot on this journey. It was therapeutic. I hope you experienced as much joy reading this book as I had writing it. I wrote this for you, for all of you. I'm getting old, but I don't feel like it because of all the young energy I receive from the youth all around the world. I never thought in a million years that I would be doing this ten, hell, even five years ago. I've been truly blessed, and my sincere goal is to bless you. I want you to find the Love you've always dreamed of. I want people to walk away with some knowledge and insight on the spirit and a newfound Love for all things.

I have no regrets in life whatsoever. Even the negative parts of my life are all a part of the play. I learned that writing a book is probably one of the hardest tasks I ever had to accomplish. I mean, life is a journey. Writing a book is an adventure. I cried, I laughed, and I evolved, all while writing this book. The process is enlightening, and I hope and pray that you are enlightened as well. I just played my part.

My Guide to Love & Romance

God willing, you'll be seeing me on my own show in 2014 called *Mama's House*. So stay tuned for that. If you're out shopping you might see my Pum-Kash line of candles, perfume, cologne, and lip-gloss. Or my Psychotic vodka, or Psychotic fashion. Feel free to purchase something to help a sista out.

With all that being said, it's been real. Thank you for tuning in to *Mama Jones' Guide to Love & Romance*. God Bless you. My final advice to all the young men and women of the world is: Love one another from the heart. Look toward the future with positivity and know that you're the ones that can change the world for the greater good. Ciao!

Check List: Questions

- ☐ What inspired you to write this book at this time?
- ☐ The question many readers ask before buying a book is "What makes you the authority on the topic?" How would you answer this question?
- ☐ How about if you use a powerful subtitle?
- ☐ What will the reader gain from reading this book?
- ☐ There are lots of books on relationships. What makes yours different?
- ☐ What absolutely convinced you that you had to write this book?
- ☐ Give our readers three important tips or strategies from the book?
- ☐ What is the most important way your book helps your readers?
- ☐ If someone read your book and sent you an email to thank you, what would you want them to say about your book and how it helped them?
- ☐ What comes next for Mama Jones?

Mama Jones
My Guide to Love & Romance

☐ What are some parting thoughts you would like to share?

254

REFERENCES

Bureau of Justice Statistics (BJS). Prison inmates at midyear 2009 – Statistical tables.
Retrieved September 11, 2013 from
http://www.bjs.gov/index.cfm?ty=pbdetail&iid=2200

Copen, CE, Daniels K, Vespa J, Mosher WD. *First marriages in the United States: Data from 2006–2010 National Survey of Family Growth*. National health statistics reports; no 49. Hyattsville, MD: National Center for Health Statistics. 2012.

Population Reference Bureau. In U.S. a sharp increase of young men living at home. 2011.
Retrieved September 11, 2013 from
http://www.prb.org/Publications/Articles/2011/us-young-adults-living-at-home.aspx

U.S. Bureau of Labor Statistics. Employment and earnings online. (January 2011).
Retrieved September 11, 2013 from
http://www.bls.gov/opub/ee

Mama Jones
My Guide to Love & Romance

STUDY GUIDE:

MAMA JONES: MY GUIDE TO LOVE & ROMANCE

Based on your knowledge of Mama Jones, book, quiz yourself or have in-depth group discussions on these topics, which are addressed in the book. Answer key is provided.

Mama Jones
My Guide to Love & Romance

1. What is the overall message Mama Jones shares with her readers about her book?
2. How important is spirituality in a relationship? Please elaborate.
3. Is love a New York state of mind, or is love something everyone is striving for in a relationship? How has your understanding of love been enhanced by Mama Jones' sound advice?
4. What is the old fashioned advice that Mama Jones received from her late grandmother which gives food for thought?
5. Statistically speaking, what percentage of Black women are married?
6. What makes Mama Jones qualified to give advice? Please elaborate, based on what you have learned from her book.
7. What is the best way to prevent becoming a sex slave to men? Answer in your own words.
8. What has been the impact of social media on Love & Romance?
9. What is Mama Jones' definition of the Lady Code?
10. What is Mama Jones' stand on domestic violence?
11. How many months does Mama Jones recommend that couples wait before having sex? Why?
12. Which animals does Mama Jones compare men and women to? Why does she use these analogies?

My Guide to Love & Romance

ANSWER KEY:

1. That it is important to be in love before you can create romance.
2. Very important. God is love. Without God there is no love.
3. According to Mama Jones, successful relationships are loving relationships.
4. Love is not supposed to hurt. When you love yourself, a man will love you.
5. Studies indicate that 26 percent are currently married, which is 6 percent less than Black men who are married.
6. Mama Jones is a survivor of life and her life experiences have given her wisdom and knowledge on love, romance, and relationships.
7. Use your feminine power.
8. Social media is so hyper-sexual that it takes away from Love & Romance.
9. They are the rules and regulations of being a real lady. She lists ten of them.
10. A real man won't hit a woman. Only a coward would hit a woman.
11. She recommends waiting at least six months to a year.
12. Mama Jones compares men with dogs and women with the feline creatures, cats. She uses the analogy to show the nature of a man and a woman. A male dog humps

several female dogs just as a man tries to have sex with as many women as he can. Women tend to be more graceful and sleek and sneaky like a cat.